TIED ON

THE COWBOY'S DEVOTIONAL

TIED ON
THE COWBOY'S DEVOTIONAL

BEAU HAGUE

Copyright © 2015 by Beau Hague

All rights reserved. No part of this publication may be reproduced, distributed, or transmitted in any form or by any means, including photocopying, recording, or other electronic or mechanical methods, without the prior written permission of the publisher, except in the case of brief quotations embodied in critical reviews and certain other noncommercial uses permitted by copyright law. For permission requests, write to the publisher at the address below.

Fedd Books
P.O. Box 341973
Austin, TX 78734
www.thefeddagency.com

Published in association with The Fedd Agency, Inc., a literary agency.

Unless otherwise indicated, Scripture quotations are taken from the *Holy Bible, New International Version*®, NIV®. Copyright © 1973, 1978, 1984, 2011 by Biblica, Inc.™ Used by permission of Zondervan. All rights reserved worldwide. www.zondervan.com. The "NIV" and "New International Version" are trademarks registered in the United States Patent and Trademark Office by Biblica, Inc.

Scripture quotations marked [NLT] are taken from the *Holy Bible*, New Living Translation, copyright ©1996, 2004, 2007, 2013 by Tyndale House Foundation. Used by permission of Tyndale House Publishers, Inc., Carol Stream, Illinois 60188. All rights reserved.

Scripture quotations marked [NASB] are from the New American Standard Bible®,Copyright © 1960, 1962, 1963, 1968, 1971, 1972, 1973, 1975, 1977, 1995 by The Lockman Foundation. Used by permission.

Scripture quotations are from The Holy Bible, English Standard Version® (ESV®), copyright © 2001 by Crossway, a publishing ministry of Good News Publishers. Used by permission. All rights reserved.

Lonesome Dove directed by Wincer Simon (CBS. 1989.), Television.

Tombstone directed by George P. Cosmatos (Hollywood Pictures. 1993.), DVD.

Cover Photo by Beau Hague/H Brand Photography

ISBN: 978-1-943217-19-9
eISBN: 978-1-943217-20-5

Printed in the United States of America
First Edition 15 14 13 10 09 / 10 9 8 7 6 5 4 3 2 1

*To my parents Kent and Crickette Hague.
Their love and commitment to Jesus has
been my greatest influence.*

CONTENTS

Introduction *13*

IT'S A TIMED EVENT 23
Week 1 *(James 4:13-17)*

DIPPING VATS 27
Week 2 *(Colossians 3:13)*

A COWBOY'S TREASURE 30
Week 3 *(Matthew 6:19-20-33)*

A HEALTHY FEAR OF HORSES 34
Week 4 *(Psalm 112:1)*

A MUDDY MESS 37
Week 5 *(2 Corinthians 5:17)*

BOMBPROOF HORSE 39
Week 6 *(Psalm 51:10-13)*

BRANDED 42
Week 7 *(Ephesians 1:13-14)*

CHOICES 45
Week 8 *(Genesis 2:17)*

CIRCLE THE WAGONS 48
Week 9 *(James 4:7)*

CIRCLES MAKE STRAIGHT LINES 50
Week 10 *(Proverbs 3:6)*

COWBOY'S TONGUE 53
Week 11 *(James 3:7-10)*

COW-TIPPING 56
Week 12 *(1 Samuel 16:7)*

CREEK PIT 59
Week 13 *(Psalm 40:1-3)*

DAY-WORKING WITH DAVID 62
Week 14 *(Psalm 40:3)*

DON'T LET DEATH LOSS DEFINE YOUR HERD 65
Week 15 *(Philippians 4:8)*

DON'T RUN 'EM TOO FAR 68
Week 16 *(Jeremiah 17:14)*

END OF THE ROPE 71
Week 17 *(Philippians 4:19)*

FORWARD MOTION 74
Week 18 *(Ecclesiastes 4:9-10)*

FROM THE PIT TO THE PLATFORM 77
Week 19 (Romans 8:28)

GIVING CREDIT WHERE CREDIT IS DUE 80
Week 20 (Proverbs 3:6)

GREEDY COWBOY 82
Week 21 (Colossians 3:5)

HAPPY TRIALS 85
Week 22 (James 1:12)

HAVE YOU BEEN CASTRATED? 87
Week 23 (1 Corinthians 6:13-14)

HESITATING GETS YOU HURT 90
Week 24 (Matthew 14:26-29)

HIS ANIMALS COME FIRST 93
Week 25 (Matthew 6:33)

HURRY UP AND WAIT 96
Week 26 (Psalm 27:14)

I'M YOUR HUCKLEBERRY 99
Week 27 (John 15:12-14)

JAKE AND JUDAS 102
Week 28 (John 12:4-6)

LEARNING FROM BETTER HORSEMEN *105*
Week 29 *(Proverbs 3:5)*

LONG LIVE COWBOYS *108*
Week 30 *(Hebrews 13:8)*

MORE HORSE *111*
Week 31 *(Ephesians 3:20)*

NO NEED FOR A NIGHT LATCH *113*
Week 32 *(Proverbs 3:5-6)*

PREPARED TO DRAG *116*
Week 33 *(Psalm 37:7)*

RIDING SHOTGUN *118*
Week 34 *(1 Corinthians 16:13)*

THE BIG DRIVE *121*
Week 35 *(Matthew 28:16-20)*

SAVED BY THE CAKE WAGON *124*
Week 36 *(John 8:12)*

SAVING THE BEST FOR LAST *127*
Week 37 *(Galatians 6:4-5)*

TAKE GROUND *130*
Week 38 *(Joshua 1:9)*

THE BULL RIDER'S ARMOR 133
Week 39 *(Ephesians 6:13-17)*

THE BUCKLE 136
Week 40 *(James 1:12)*

THE CORNER POST 138
Week 41 *(Hebrews 11:1)*

THE FLY OF LIFE 141
Week 42 *(1 Corinthians 16:14)*

THE GREAT HANDLER 143
Week 43 *(1 John 5:12)*

THE ORDINARY COWBOY 146
Week 44 *(1 Samuel 16:11)*

THE PERFORMANCE HORSE 149
Week 45 *(Matthew 9:12-13)*

THE REAL MCCOY 151
Week 46 *(Psalm 112:1)*

LIFE'S A TWITCH 154
Week 47 *(Exodus 14:13-14)*

THE WINDMILL 157
Week 48 *(John 7:38)*

WHAT A TOOL 160
Week 49 *(John 7:38)*

WHAT MAKES YOUR CLOTHES FALL OFF............163
Week 50 *(Galatians 3:26-27)*

YOU CAN LEAD A HORSE TO WATER.................166
Week 51 *(James 1:12)*

GETTING A LITTLE WESTERN................................169
Week 52 *(Psalm 145:3)*

Notes..*172*

INTRODUCTION

This devotional has been something that God has prepared me for since I was just a young boy. From the time I was a kid, I've always loved horses and everything having to do with the lifestyle of a cowboy. I remember it like it was yesterday, my dad making a deal with me saying, "You fix all the fences and I'll buy you a horse." That's all I needed to hear, so after fixing the entire fence on our little farm in Mustang, Oklahoma, my parents bought me my first horse. His name was Baron, and he was half Quarter Horse, half Arabian. I know what you're thinking, "Nice breeding smart guy", but while Baron probably wasn't the purest bred horse, he was mine and I loved him. From that moment on I was hooked. I loved everything about having a horse. I loved the work of taking care of him, the thrill of getting to ride, the ability to bond with such

TIED ON

a cool animal, having fresh hay in the barn, and just the smell of a horse. Unfortunately, it wasn't too long after I got Baron that my dad said he had taken another job and we were moving.

But that wasn't the bad news.

What tore me up was when he said we would not be able to keep Baron because where we were moving there would be no room for him. So Baron was sold, and we moved to Duncan, Oklahoma on a street called Country Club Road. (Seriously, the name of the street was Country Club Road but just to clarify, we were too poor to become members of the *actual* Country Club.)

But I ended up loving growing up in town. We had a pretty big backyard with a pool and a volley ball court which meant we could have all our friends over in the summers and have a heck of a lot of fun. But I'd be lying if I didn't tell you that I always had this itch to be back in the country and on the back of a horse. I would go to every horse show they had in OKC. I'd go to rodeos every weekend during the summer, and I would try and find a way to get horseback every chance I could. It was also during these high-school years that God began growing my love for the church. I loved going to the youth group at our church. I loved going on mission trips and going to church camp. After graduating high-school God opened the doors for me to go to college and get my degree. It

INTRODUCTION

was while in college that I felt God's calling me to serve Him in full-time ministry. Since I was single and I liked a good adventure, I decided that if I'm going to do this full-time ministry thing, I might as well have fun at it. So, I spent a ski-season in Colorado as a missionary, working at a ski resort (because as we all know ski bunnies need Jesus too).

After that, God opened the doors for me to serve as a missionary in Israel.

That's right.

Israel…

Where Jesus grew up, walked on water, performed his ministry, died, and rose from the dead. After spending ten weeks sharing the gospel and helping churches there reach more people, I had experienced things that most Christians can only dream of. I swam in the Dead Sea, river-rafted down the Jordan River, went to the Wailing Wall, climbed Mt. Masada, rode a camel on top of the Mount of Olives, went to the garden of Gethsemane, saw the supposed sight of the tomb where they laid Jesus after he had died, and went to the town of Bethlehem where Jesus was born. Needless to say, it was an experience I will cherish for the rest of my life! After that, I came home and God opened up even more doors for me to become a youth minister. It was while serving at my first church as youth minister in Laverne, Oklahoma that

TIED ON

I was able to rekindle my love for the country. NW Oklahoma is God's country and I fell in love with the country life even more. Because the population of Laverne was pretty small and there wasn't a girl in sight that I would consider marrying, God saw fit to once again open the doors for me to serve as youth pastor in Ada, Oklahoma. It was while serving there, that I met my wife Heather (and, no, she wasn't in my youth group—she was attending college in Ada and was a part of the college ministry at the church where I served).

While I married Heather because she was beautiful, talented, and loved Jesus, it didn't hurt that her grandpa owned a farm and ranch back in Northwest Oklahoma and raised quarter horses. It was while we were still dating that I inquired about getting some colts from her grandpa. It wasn't too long after voicing my desire, that her grandpa made it possible for us to get two yearlings of our own. Since that time we've never not owned horses. After spending a few more years in youth ministry and starting a family, God called me to become a pastor of a church near where we now live, in Sharon, Oklahoma.

While serving at this little country church, I had the opportunity to raise a few more horses and fulfill my dream of working at some really great ranches and learn the fine art of cowboyin'. Out of these experiences and out of a specific calling to bring together my love

INTRODUCTION

for cowboyin' and pastorin', God called us to start a cowboy church in 2010, which we named *1000 Hills Ranch Church*. So, for the last five years, I've been able to pastor a growing, exciting, and fun cowboy church that meets in a sale barn every Sunday morning, while having the pleasure of working on some of the best ranches in Northwest Oklahoma and West Texas with some of the best cowboys the country.

It's out of these experiences of day-working and pastorin', that I've written this devotional.

From starting my own colts for the last fourteen years, to fine tuning my roping skills, to ranch rodeoin', to getting up before the sun rises and being dropped off by the cowboys at the back of some pretty big pastures and gathering hundreds of pairs while day-working, to dragging hundreds of calves to the branding pot—I'm having the time of my life!

I truly believe that the men who get to cowboy for a living, own a ranch, raise horses, live in the country, or just have the dream of doing so, will relate to or be able to live vicariously through the adventures and stories that are written on these pages. I also believe that if a guy will take the time to read the scripture that is on these pages, answer the questions, and prayerfully commit to apply the truths found in this book, their lives will be changed through the power of God! Why do I believe this? It's

TIED ON

because through the power of the Holy Spirit and the truths found in the Bible God has changed me and grown me in my ride with Him!

TIED ON

In our part of the country, when it comes to roping cattle out in the pasture or in the brandin' pen, a good hand will typically "tie on". Whether it's roping a yearling that needs to be doctored, catching wild cattle, or dragging calves to the ground crew to be worked, being tied on better assures that whatever you've roped, won't get away.

I like to tie on, but I don't do it because I think I'm a good hand, I prefer to tie on cause I'm not too proficient at getting my dally (you cowboys that don't team rope feel me don't you?).

If you're not savvy to cowboyin' then you may be thinking, "What the heck do you mean when you say *tied on or dally* for that matter?" To be *tied on* means that you have your rope either tied to the saddle horn by a couple of small loops at the end of your rope, placed over your saddle-horn and tied with a knot, or secured to the saddle horn by looping your rope over the horn and sucking it tight with a *horn knot* (a circular tool made of some chain links or braided rope that you loop the end of your rope through to be able to cinch it tight to your saddle-horn).

INTRODUCTION

So, when you *tie on,* it's just like the term implies-- you're tied on. If you go and rope a 1,200 lb. momma cow, she is essentially tied on to your saddle by your rope. For most cowboys, while they would say being tied onto a crazy momma cow or a soggy yearling is just a part of the job, they would also say that is pretty exciting and fun. When you're tied on, unless your rope breaks or your saddle-horn breaks, you're not going anywhere without that cow going with you.

As followers of Jesus, I believe that we should be *tied on* to our Savior, Jesus Christ. We are to be so tight with God that it feels that we are tied together. We get tied on to Christ when we surrender our lives to Him by accepting Him as our Savior and Lord. From that point on the Bible teaches us that we will always be together. There may be times that we are at the end of the rope getting choked down, but we usually find ourselves in this situation because we are fighting His leading. But when we submit to His leading and obey Him we can enjoy a pretty amazing ride together. I also believe that as committed followers of Jesus, we should be *tied on to the Truths and teachings of the Word of God.* When we tie on to God's Word, the Bible, and the principles found in its pages, we have the privilege of living a pretty exciting life!

This devotional is meant to tie you to our Savior and my prayer is that you will enjoy reading about some of

TIED ON

the exciting experiences that I've had cowboyin', pastorin' a cowboy church, raising horses and my family. But most importantly I hope that you will tie on to our amazing Savior and the truths that He has given us in the Bible.

CHEW ON THIS

One of my favorite verses in the Bible is Joshua 1:8 that says, "Do not let this book of the law depart from your mouth; meditate on it day and night, that you may be careful to do everything written in it—then you will be prosperous and successful." My dad calls it the "key to success," because this verse tells us to meditate on the Word of God.

What does it mean to meditate on God's Word? I'll illustrate it by using the example of a cow chewing its cud. A cow has four stomachs, and what it does, is it will graze out in the pasture eating grass or hay. Once she does that, a cow will usually lay down and chew its cud. This process includes them chewing the grass up, swallowing it, getting some nutrients from the forage, and then regurgitating it up and chewing it again. They will do this many times and each time they chew, regurgitate, and swallow their food, they are gaining the nutrients from the food and growing.

Meditating on the Word of God is just like chewing cud.

INTRODUCTION

We take in God's Word into our heart, mind, and soul by reading it. Once we've taken it in, we are told to meditate or chew on its truth and allow it to fill our heart. If we chew on God's Word through the process of reading it, thinking on it, and applying its powerful truths, it will help us grow in our spiritual lives each day! Psalm 1:1-2 says, "Blessed is the one who does not walk in step with the wicked or stand in the way that sinners take or sit in the company of mockers, but whose delight is in the law of the Lord, and who meditates on his law day and night." My prayer is that you would be blessed and grow in your life with Christ as you tie on to Him and chew on His Word daily.

PRAYER

Prayer is the privilege of every follower of Christ to talk personally to God. At the end of each devotion, you will be given a suggested prayer. I hope that you will tap into the power of God by praying these prayers of commitment. Remember, if we want to experience what only God can do, then we have to ask. Psalm 116:1-2 says, "I love the Lord because he hears my voice and my prayer for mercy. Because he bends down to listen, I will pray as long as I have breath."

WEEK 1

IT'S A TIMED EVENT

JAMES 4:1-17

Now listen, you who say, "Today or tomorrow we will go to this or that city, spend a year there, carry on business and make money." Why, you do not even know what will happen tomorrow. What is your life? You are a mist that appears for a little while and then vanishes. Instead, you ought to say, "If it is the Lord's will, we will live and do this or that." As it is, you boast in your arrogant schemes. All such boasting is evil. If anyone, then, knows the good they ought to do and doesn't do it, it is sin for them.

I love ranch rodeos. The events at a ranch rodeo are patterned after the real life jobs that a cowboy would perform every day on the ranch—from branding calves, gathering strays, or sorting and penning cattle, to even having to catch a momma cow that won't let her newborn calf milk

TIED ON

and having to milk her by hand to get that baby some milk. The only difference is each event is a timed event.

Like the timed events in a PRCA rodeo, ranch rodeos are all about getting the fastest time. The fastest winning time over all four events wins the entire rodeo. But there is another factor that comes into play—most of the events have a time limit. If you miss a few loops in an event, your worry isn't so much about getting the fastest time. It's worrying about running out of time. If you've ever been in a ranch rodeo, you know how short that two-minute time limit can be when you're hustling to get a time.

The same is true in this rodeo called *life*. The Bible is clear that life is a timed event and whether we like it or not we are competing against the clock. One day the buzzer is going to sound and we are either going to die or the Lord is going to come back. Either way life as we know it will be over.

The older I get the shorter life seems.

Today's passage proves this to be true when it says in verse 14, "You are a mist that appears for a little while and then vanishes." This verse confirms that this life is short. And the proof is all around us; from a few hairs turning gray (or for some of you turning loose) to our children growing up way too fast, life proves to be short.

Knowing this we need to make the best run we can in this arena before the buzzer sounds and time runs out.

IT'S A TIMED EVENT

What does it take to make a great run? Well, the first thing we have to do is enter the arena. How do we get into the arena? We have to enter through the gate. Who is the gate? Jesus. In John 10:9 Jesus tells the people, "I am the gate; whoever enters through me will be saved. They will come in and go out, and find pasture." Not only do we get to enter into the arena of God's family through Jesus, we get to spend eternity in the arena of heaven.

So the question we must answer is: What should our response be to getting to enter into these arenas?

The answer: It's to get mounted and ride for Him! Sadly, many Christians enter the gate and head straight to the fence, tie their horse to the rail, and head straight for the stands. Truth is, these folks may make it into the arena of heaven, but will never make a winning run here on earth if they don't get in the arena of life and ride for God's glory and the good of others!

CHEW ON THIS
Are you aware that this life is a timed event? Are you making this "run in life" with Christ by your side or have you not entered through the gate named Jesus?

PRAYER
Lord, I want to make this run with you. I give you my heart

TIED ON

and I ask that you would save me from my sin. I want to enter into the arena of heaven someday, but in the meantime I want to make a winning run here on earth! Help me not to be a spectator, but to enter the gate and ride for you. It's in your holy name I pray, Amen.

WEEK 2

DIPPING VATS

COLOSSIANS 3:13

Bear with each other and forgive one another if any of you has a grievance against someone. Forgive as the Lord forgave you.

In the 1860s and 1870s, Texas was divided into two camps. South Texas Cattlemen who needed to drive their cattle north to the railheads, and the North Texas Cattlemen who stood armed and ready to stop them. Why did the North Cattlemen want to stop the South's cattle from coming across their land? Because the southern cattle of Texas had what was called "Texas Fever." This disease was a death wish for any non-affected cattle that came into contact with a bovine that carried the disease. After figuring out that ticks were spreading the infection, biologists came up with an insecticide that would kill it. Along with spraying the pastures with the insecticide, the infected cattle were run through "dipping vats" and drenched with the insecticide. By running the cattle through these vats the disease was eradicated, therefore stopping one of the deadliest diseases in history.

On this trail of life, sometimes we get infested by ticks of sin. Ticks of sexual immorality, ticks of pride, and ticks of envy, are just some of the ticks of sin we find sucking the life out of us. I've found that just like those cows had to be drenched in the vats of insecticide, we too must be drenched in the vats of forgiveness! By walking through these vats we can be eradicated from the sickness of sin.

For you, it may be that you need to go through the vat of forgiving others. It's not until we walk through this vat that the ticks of unforgiveness, anger, resentment, and bitterness can be eradicated from our lives.

CHEW ON THIS
Are you walking around with the ticks of sin sucking the life right out of you? What's it going to take to get you to walk through God's dipping vat of forgiveness and eradicate your sins? Do you need to walk through the dipping vat of forgiving others?

DIPPING VATS

PRAYER

Thank you, Jesus, for your power to eradicate sin. Please reveal to me the sin that needs to be eradicated from my life and lead me through your vat of forgiveness. Also, please help me to forgive those who have done me wrong. It's in your holy name I pray, Amen.

WEEK 3

A COWBOY'S TREASURE

MATTHEW 6:19-20:33

Do not store up for yourselves treasures on earth, where moths and vermin destroy, and where thieves break in and steal. But store up for yourselves treasures in heaven, where moths and vermin do not destroy, and where thieves do not break in and steal. For where your treasure is, there your heart will be also ... But seek first his kingdom and his righteousness, and all these things will be given to you as well.

My wife and I leave our kids with their grandparents and take a week-long vacation every year to relax, re-connect, and just have fun. Each year on this vacation, we go to the WRCA Finals in Amarillo. One of my favorite parts of the World Championship Ranch Rodeo is the Cowboy Trade

A COWBOY'S TREASURE

and Trappings Show. At this show you can sell, trade, or swap every kind of cowboy gear imaginable. From bits, to chaps, to hats, to saddles, to art, to chutes, and even trailers ... it's all there. In the cowboy culture these things are often referred to as "*trappings*". These trappings could be fancy gear that a guy might hang on the wall and admire, or they can be just simple gear that a cowboy would use at work every day. For many cowboys, these trappings are their treasure! I've seen many a cowboy, including myself, spend more money on these trappings than on anything else they own. I for one love owning and using nice handmade gear because it holds up longer and you save money in the long run by buying quality gear that will last a lifetime. (At least that's what I tell my wife when I want to buy something that's a little expensive—wink, wink.)

If you were to look at what the Bible says about the trappings and treasures of this world, you may be surprised to find that owning nice things is not sinful. In the book of Genesis, God says, "Everything I made at creation is good!" So if God himself thinks it's good, wouldn't it be foolish for us to say that it's not?

1 Timothy 6:17 says that God "richly provides us with everything for our enjoyment." This verse shows us that God has blessed us with the things of this world for our enjoyment and pleasure! So the question you might be

TIED ON

asking is, "What makes the trappings and treasures of this world sinful?" Our key verse shows us the answer. It tells us that if we will find out where our heart is, we will find out where our treasure is. If our heart is set more on the trappings of this world—if our minds are controlled by the things that we own and our trappings lead us to worry or stress—then we may have our hearts set more on the things of this world then on the things of God.

So, how do we keep from being trapped by the treasures of this world? Matthew 6:33 gives the answer. It says to "seek first God's kingdom and His righteousness..." and this will assure that our trappings are always kept in the right place. (Not to mention he will give us what we need and from my own experience He often times even blesses us with what we want).

How do we seek Him first? Before we make a decision to buy something, we pray for God's approval. We practice delayed gratification, rather than instant gratification. Another instance that we should always keep God first, is before we spend our paycheck. The moment we get it, we should give a portion back to the Lord through our tithes and offerings. This helps us keep Him first in our heart, our mind, *and* in our wallet.

A COWBOY'S TREASURE

CHEW ON THIS

Where is your heart? Where is your mind? What do you find yourself spending most of your time, money, and energy on? Is your mind set more on material things that you have or want, or are you focused on the things that you want to accomplish for God? Remember, it's not wrong to own things as long as they don't own you! And what truly owns our mind and heart, is where our treasure is!

PRAYER

God, thank you for blessing me with worldly treasures for my pleasure! Please help me to enjoy the things you've given me but help my treasure be found in you and the things you treasure. It's in your holy name I pray, Amen.

WEEK 4

A HEALTHY FEAR OF HORSES

PSALM 112:1
Praise the Lord. Blessed is the man who fears the Lord, who finds great delight in his commands.

I want to teach my children to have a healthy fear of horses. So, starting at a young age, I've tried to share with them that horses are powerful, strong, and can really get you hurt if you don't respect them and pay attention. My kids know when they walk behind a horse, to stay close to the horse and put their hands on him to let him know that they're there. They know to be gentle around the horse—not to be loud and crazy. They know how to lead a horse from the side and not from the front because, in case the horse jumps forward, they are not going to get ran over but will be safely to the side. My hopes in instilling this healthy fear is that it will keep them from getting hurt and that they will learn to have fun and stay safe around their horse.

I believe that in the same way we are to have a healthy fear of horses, as Christ followers we ought to possess a healthy fear of God! God is all powerful. He is strong and mighty. He is the creator of the world. He can keep us from getting hurt, and if we fear Him and honor Him, He will lead us to victory over sin and death! I also believe that we should pass this holy fear to our kids. Just like I teach my kids how to respect the power of a horse, I have to be intentional about teaching them to have respect for the power that God has. I want them to know that he is mighty and that He is all they need to get them through the trials and temptations of life.

I want them to understand that to fear the Lord doesn't mean we have this trembling fear of His wrath or punishment, although his wrath and punishment are real, but a holy fear and reverence.

As a Father myself, it is my calling to lead my family to fear God! If my kids don't revere Him, honor Him, and love Him, then they are going to face a lot more trials and trouble in this world!

CHEW ON THIS
Do you have a healthy fear of God? In what ways can you show God and others you have a healthy fear of God? Are

TIED ON

you passing that holy fear to others?

PRAYER

God, help me to continue to develop a healthy fear of you. Help me to honor and respect you because I am in awe of your majesty. Help me to live my life in a way that helps others to have a healthy fear of you as well. In Jesus name I pray, Amen.

WEEK 5

A MUDDY MESS

2 CORINTHIANS 5:17
Therefore, if anyone is in Christ, the new creation has come: The old has gone, the new is here!

We had a ranch rodeo not long ago and because it had rained all weekend, the arena was a muddy mess! We were covered in mud, from the top of our hats to the bottom of our boots! I remember that I drove home that night half naked because my clothes were too far gone and I just needed to throw them away (sorry for putting that picture in your mind). While we had a great time and even won a prize that weekend, there was nothing better than coming home from that muddy night, taking a shower, and putting on something clean and new!

Spiritually speaking, when we put our faith in Christ, He takes our old dirty clothes of sin and shame and throws them away. He takes our past, our failures, our

TIED ON

filth, our sin, and gets rid of them, and then, He gives us a new set of clothes to wear! What do these new clothes look like? They are clothes of righteousness. Through our acceptance of Jesus' forgiveness we are given the power to live a right life. We are able to say no the filth of sin and walk a clean, upright life for His glory. Will we ever get muddy in sin again? Sure, but because of Christ's forgiveness, we have the ability to be made clean each day as we turn to Him for cleansing. Not to mention when we get to heaven God will welcome us into heaven not because of our own ability to live a righteous life, but because he will see the clothes that His Son gave to us and tell us to come on in. Thank you, Jesus, for such a wonderful gift!

CHEW ON THIS
Have you traded in your clothes of sin for the clothes of righteousness by accepting Christ's forgiveness? If not, ask God to forgive you of your sin and make you a new creation!

PRAYER
Lord, thank you for offering a way for me to be made new. Please wash me clean and help me live a new life in you. It's in your holy name I pray, Amen.

WEEK 6

BOMBPROOF HORSE

PSALM 51:10-13

Create in me a pure heart O God, and renew a steadfast spirit within me. Do not cast me from your presence or take your Holy Spirit from me. Restore to me the joy of your salvation and grant me a willing spirit, to sustain me. Then I will teach transgressors your ways, and sinners will turn back to you.

In today's horse market, most horses aren't worth much. Sure, there are some winning and producing sires, some proven rodeo horses that can be worth a lot of money, and even some respected ranches that can seem to sell their ranch horses for a decent profit, but for the most part, the horse market is dead.

There is, however, one type of horse that will always

TIED ON

be marketable, and that's a *bombproof* kid horse. What's a bombproof horse? It's usually a retired rodeo horse or seasoned ranch horse that has spent its life in the arena or on the ranch and is being retired from the long days of working for a living. This horse is a horse with a good foundation. A horse that has had lots of wet saddle blankets, has been to town, or in rare cases just possesses that calmness about him is a "bombproof" horse. A horse like this is a hot commodity! Typically they're not for sale, but if you do ever find one for sale, you better be ready to pay some bucks for them, cause they're not cheap!

Of course, all horses, even a "bombproof" horse, will at some point in their life take a bad step, get in a bind, or not want to cooperate—at any age and at any time, a horse can make a mistake—the difference, however, between a bombproof horse and a regular horse, is a bombproof horse rarely makes these mistakes.

Just like there are bombproof horses, there are also bombproof believers. Sure they are still sinners, but their sin is rare. Why? Because their faith is strong! Like a bombproof horse, sin is the *exception* not the norm. There are cowboys and cowgirls with knowledge of the Bible and these are Christians that aren't afraid to share their faith! How does one become a bombproof believer? We must pray today's verse. We must pray for the Lord to give us a pure heart, renew our spirit, grant us the joy of

BOMBPROOF HORSE

His salvation, and therefore, give us the authority to tell others about Jesus and see their lives changed! The more we grow on this trail with Christ, the more we become bombproof believers.

CHEW ON THIS
Would others say you are a bombproof believer? What are some things that are keeping you from having the influence you need to help lead others into a relationship with Christ? How can you be more of a witness in the world?

PRAYER
Lord, help me to become a bombproof believer. Help sin be rare in my life. Create in me a pure heart and help me to tell others about you more often. It's in your holy name I pray, Amen.

WEEK 7

BRANDED

EPHESIANS 1:13-14

And you also were included in Christ when you heard the word of Truth, the gospel of your salvation. Having believed, you were marked in Him with a seal, the promised Holy Spirit, who is a deposit guaranteeing our inheritance until the redemption of those who are God's possession—to the praise of His glory.

Wild mustangs are a beautiful animal that are symbols of the West, and if you've ever been around them, you will notice that all of them have a very distinguishing freeze brand on their neck. I've always wondered how and why they were branded the way they are. Turns out, that the BLM (Bureau of Land Management) is responsible for most of the wild horses in the U.S. and in 1978, the BLM came up with a way to identify these horses by freeze branding them. They use a system called an Alpha Angle

BRANDED

System, which is a series of straight lines and angles that are branded onto the left side of the mustang's neck. This brand is almost impossible to alter or remove. In the brand you have the registering organization (U.S. Government), the year of birth, and the registration number (this number varies according to the state in which it was born or caught). What does this brand show us? It is a brand of authenticity—it identifies the horse as an official wild horse and it also shows ownership by the US Government.

Similar to how I wondered how the wild mustangs were branded, many people wonder how they too can be distinguished as a follower of the Lord and wonder what His brand looks like. What is the Lord's brand of authenticity?

The answers to these questions can be found in today's verse. It shows us that we can be branded for the Lord by hearing the truth and believing it. The truth is that Jesus died for our sins so that we can be forgiven and have eternal life—and once we place our faith in Christ we are branded. We are branded with an internal and eternal brand called the Holy Spirit.

CHEW ON THIS

Have you been branded for the Lord? Have you confessed your sins to the Lord and received His Holy Spirit as your

TIED ON

brand? How are you allowing the Holy Spirit to work in and through you?

PRAYER
Lord, thank you for dying on the cross so that by confessing you as my Savior, I can be forgiven and branded by you. Help me to share this with others so they can be branded by you as well. In Jesus name I pray, Amen.

WEEK 8

CHOICES

GENESIS 2:17
. . . but you must not eat from the tree of the knowledge of good and evil, for when you eat from it you will certainly die.

If you were born in the last fifty years, you probably are familiar with the great George Jones. Songs like, "Why Baby Why," "White Lightening," "Hold On," and "He Stopped Loving Her Today," were among his greatest hits. But if you weren't keen on country music at the time, you probably didn't know about the life that George lived off stage. In his personal life, George had been married and divorced three times, one of those being to the famous Tammy Wynette, before marrying his current wife, Nancy. He also had an addiction to alcohol. While drinking whiskey like it was water, he got into drugs, blew pretty much all of his money, and went totally bankrupt, (not to mention, he was a part of over a hundred

TIED ON

lawsuits and missed fifty shows in just one year, earning him the nickname "No Show Jones"). The story goes, that at the concerts he did make it to, the lead guitarist would stand on one side of him and the bass player on the other, just to keep him from falling over in a drunken stupor. He was on a tragic path to self-destruction.

But, in 1999, after a horrific car accident, Jones finally got sober, and not long after, recorded the song "Choices." In the song Jones sings, "I had choices since the day I was born, there were voices that told me right from wrong. If I had listened, then I wouldn't be here today, living and dying with the choices I've made." Looking back, Jones realized that every road he went down, good or bad, all start with a choice.

Everybody has choices to make. Why does God give us the power of choice? Because He loves us. He doesn't want to force us to love him, because that wouldn't really be love. As we read in today's Scripture, Adam and Eve had a choice too. They could choose to obey God and not eat the forbidden fruit or choose to disobey and bring sin into the world. If you read the rest of their story, you will know that they made the wrong choice, and it is because of that choice that we have sin today. The truth is, we too have a choice to make. We can choose to obey Christ and receive rewards, or we can choose to disobey and receive the consequences or our sin. I praise God for His promise that if we place our trust in His Son, we can have all the power we need to make right choices.

CHEW ON THIS
What road do you find yourself on today, and how have your choices determined where you find yourself? What wrong choices have you made already that you need to repent? Are you making choices that honor God?

PRAYER
Lord, please help me to make choices that honor you. Help me to remember that my choices affect not only myself, but others as well. In Jesus name I pray, Amen.

WEEK 9

CIRCLE THE WAGONS

JAMES 4:7
Submit yourselves, then, to God. Resist the devil, and he will flee from you.

Back in the days of the Wild West, where you had wagon robbers with pistols and Native Americans with knives and bows waiting for anyone who came across their land, there was a phrase that the travelers would use if there was trouble that they couldn't run from: Circle the wagons. This meant that they would put their wagons in a circle as to make a fortress. By circling the wagons, they had protection from all sides. In doing this, the travelers under attack would give themselves the protection they needed to make a stand in hopes that the enemy would give up

CIRCLE THE WAGONS

and leave.

As Christians, we are called to do the same thing as they did in the Wild West. Today's verse shows us that when the enemy attacks, we are commanded to resist him and he will flee from us. When the devil tries to get into your mind, we are told to take a stand and resist him in Jesus' name. When the devil tries to destroy your marriage, we are told to fight with the spiritual weapons of prayer and God's Word. We are not called to *circle the wagons* alone, but ask other Christians to *circle the wagons* with us so that we can win the battle even more decisively. When we have others helping us, we will find greater victory.

CHEW ON THIS
What are you facing today that makes you feel like you have to protect yourself from the enemy and *circle the wagons*? Who do you need to call up and ask to circle the wagons with you through prayer and wisdom?

PRAYER
Lord, help me to take a stand. Help me to stand firm in my faith so that I can resist the devil and watch him flee from me. Thank you for the friends that have circled the wagons with me. May I circle the wagons with them when they find themselves attacked too. It's in your holy name I pray, Amen.

WEEK 10

CIRCLES MAKE STRAIGHT LINES

PROVERBS 3:6
... and he will make your paths straight.

In my limited experience training horses, one thing I always hate is when my horse won't trot or walk in a straight line. For some reason, when you're just trying to walk straight, a young colt wants to turn, duck, and act drunk. Well, from the wisdom a trainer friend of mine gave me, I learned that to get a horse to walk, trot, or canter in a straight line, you have to ride circles. I really don't know how this works, but it does. The more you ride in circles, the straighter your horse will go when you line him out. I figure this works 'cause the colt has to learn to trust your hands to guide him around and around, and when you let him straighten out, he trusts you then too.

CIRCLES MAKE STRAIGHT LINES

The same method seems to be true in this ride with Christ. Many times, we have to ride in what seems like circles to figure out how to ride straight. The Lord does this through us having to trust Him when life throws us for a loop, when life just seems like it's taking us in circles, or when obstacles seem to get in our way. I believe that the goal of these circles in life, are to lead us to the straight path that God has for us.

Proverbs 3:5-6 says, "Trust in the Lord with all your heart, and lean not on your own understanding; in all your ways acknowledge him, and he will make your paths straight." Here, He says He will guide us, give us wisdom, and show us His plan. We must trust Him, seek His wisdom, and acknowledge Him before men. Then, He will give us a straight shot to His will and blessings.

Why does He promise to do this? Because if we are trusting and seeking Him, our path is no longer our path, but His.

CHEW ON THIS

How straight is your path? Do you feel like you're on a winding road that is leading you nowhere? Maybe you've taken a wrong turn 'cause you've tried to do things on your own. Confess and turn!

TIED ON

PRAYER

Lord, thank you for promising that if we trust and seek you, you will make our paths straight. Help me to trust you, lean on your understanding, acknowledge you and then praise you for making my paths straight. It's in your holy name I pray, Amen.

WEEK 11

COWBOY'S TONGUE

JAMES 3:7-10
All kinds of animals, birds, reptiles and creatures of the sea are being tamed and have been tamed by man, but no man can tame the tongue. It is a restless evil, full of deadly poison. With the tongue we praise our Lord and father, and with it we curse men, who have been made in God's likeness. Out of the same mouth come praise and cursing. My brothers, this should not be.

When you spend a lot of time with cowboys, you find that, like other cultures, you have varying types of personalities. For instance, you have the type of person that doesn't hold anything back! If you're not good at something, this cowboy will tell you you're not good. If you're

TIED ON

taking forever to catch in the branding pen, they may tell you you're done. If you're sorting pairs and you let a calf or two through, they may tell you to get out of the way and go get the fire started. These types talk a lot and sometimes offend others with their words. But the good thing about them is you always know where you stand with them, and I appreciate that about this type.

Then, you have the other type of cowboy that doesn't say much. He just rides quietly doing his job, but when he speaks, everyone listens. His words are softly spoken and he never raises his voice. His downfall may be that he doesn't always get the best out of his hand 'cause he's too afraid to say something. Truth is, whether a person has no filter or has too tight a filter, we can learn a lot about a man just by the words that he says or doesn't say.

Do you realize that people are listening to you and your words? If the world were to judge you by the words you use, what would they know about you? Would they say you are encouraging and uplifting? Or would they say you're crabby and always doggin' someone? Would they know that you love Jesus with all your heart? Or would they be surprised to find out that you're a Christian? See, our tongue can speak life or death, and in order to change your tongue, you have to allow God to change you from the inside out! Matthew 12:34 says, "For out of the abundance of the heart the mouth speaks." It's all about your

COWBOY'S TONGUE

heart! Jesus reminds us that what we say reveals what is in our heart! The heart is the key to right speech. We don't clean up our speech to change our heart, we change our heart to clean up our speech. When Christ is the Lord of your heart, He will be the Lord of your tongue, too. My prayer is that you and I would give God our heart and our tongue each day and ask Him to use it to be a blessing to others and to honor Him.

CHEW ON THIS
What do your words say about who you are or who's you are? Is God the Lord of your heart and your tongue? What are three things you need to change about the way you speak?

PRAYER
Lord, please be the Lord of my heart and my tongue. I pray that people would know I love you by the words I say. It's in your holy name I pray, Amen.

WEEK 12

COW - TIPPING

1 Samuel 16:7
But the Lord said to Samuel, "Do not consider his appearance or his height, for I have rejected him. The Lord does not look at the things man looks at. Man looks at the outward appearance, but the Lord looks at the heart."

If you're like me, you always wear your cowboy hat no matter where you go. I wear a custom-made cowboy hat with a 5" brim cause I just like the look of a bigger brim. (Not to mention I think a bigger hat makes you look slimmer, and that's always good thing when you like to eat too many donuts like I do.) But what you may notice is that in many cases your cowboy hat makes other people feel uncomfortable. For some reason they don't know what to say to you. They may even think you aren't as smart as they are or as successful as them. Sadly, I find that many cowboys feel this way at church.

COW - TIPPING

A lot of cowboys feel rejected by Christians and churches because they may not have the right kind of clothes, drive a dirty old ranch truck with a beat up cake box, and have a Cowdog tied to the spare tire on the bed. So, when they show up at some churches they feel like they don't belong and they don't like going to church. Because I know this is true, I've made it a part of my life's purpose to do some cow-tipping. In our cowboy church, we've done our best to tip these kinds of "sacred cows" over and not let them get back up.

As we read in today's verse, God doesn't care one bit about our outward appearance. I've never read a story in the Bible where Jesus said to his disciples, "Clean up before you can follow me. Or, "You guys smell like fish. Go change your clothes and put on these white robes and then you can be fishers of men." Do we need to take care of ourselves and have personal hygiene? Yes, please do! But to judge someone based on their appearance ... come on now! Remember that God is not looking for those who look the part, but those who *play* the part.

Jesus himself didn't look the part of the King of Kings. Why? Because He was more concerned with pleasing His Father than pleasing others! God is looking for the same in us! He's looking for those with a heart for Him, those who love Him and will give Him their all!

TIED ON

CHEW ON THIS
What do you worry about more, the outside of a man or the inside? What does the church you go to feel like for those that may wear a cowboy hat or have poo on their boots?

PRAYER
God help me to not judge others on their outward appearance. May all people of all walks of life feel comfortable in their own boots as they walk into our churches. It's in your holy name I pray, Amen.

WEEK 13

CREEK PIT

PSALM 40:1-3

I waited patiently for the Lord; he turned to me and heard my cry. He lifted me out of the slimy pit, out of the mud and mire; he set my feet on a rock and gave me a firm place to stand. He put a new song in my mouth, a hymn of praise to our God. Many will see and fear and put their trust in the Lord.

My friend Jason Taylor (Pastor of Bar None Cowboy Church) once told a story about him having to chase down a yearling that had gotten out and was on his neighbor. While blowing to this yearling and riding wide-open he found himself coming up on a creek, and as he reached the bank, his horse tried to check up and stop, but Jason just kept pushing her until they ended up jumping right into the creek. When the horse tried to make it up the other side, she slipped and fell back down into the water.

TIED ON

Jason slid off the side, but found himself caught underwater in the rope. He told me he remembered thinking, *"If that horse gets out of here and doesn't stop, I'm going to get drug to death."* As it turned out, the horse swam back to the bank and slowly got out of the water, while at the same time pulling Jason out. Once they both were out of the water his horse just stopped. "She saved my life, even though it was me that got us both in that mess," he told me.

Similar to Jason's horse, God tries to keep us out of the pits of life. The Holy Spirit warns us ... *"Slow down", "Don't do that", "Get out of here."* But we just keep spurring, and we bale off into a pit. But the same God who gives us a choice to obey Him or not, is the God who, like that good horse, can pull us out of the pit! We must simply put our trust in God and follow Him!

When we do find ourselves in the pit, God desires our cry for Him! Crying out to Him means we are declaring we can't get out on our own, and that we desperately need the Lord. So many times when we are in the pit we cry out for help from things other than God such as money or a friend. While those things may be helpful, our cry needs to go to God! Only He can truly rescue us from the pits of life.

CHEW ON THIS
What creek do you find yourself in today? When you hear the Holy Spirit, do you listen and heed His warning? Or

CREEK PIT

do you keep spurring and land in the pit? Even if the pit you're in is your own fault, God wants to help you out of it! Cry out to Him today!

PRAYER

God, I know that you are in the pit rescuin' business! I need your forgiveness so I'm crying out to you today. I trust you, and I choose to follow you. Thank you for delivering me from this pit! It's in your holy name I pray, Amen.

WEEK 14

DAY-WORKING WITH DAVID

PSALM 40:3

He put a new song in my mouth, a hymn of praise to our God.

Not too long ago, my friend David called asking if I could do some day-work for him. When we got to the ranch that morning, most of the cows were already caught and in the corrals, but we were there to find some rogue momma cows that just wouldn't come in. The pasture we were in was a few hundred acres of nothing but thick brush and cedars. Needless to say, it wasn't the easiest place to find cattle. After searching for hours, enduring the Oklahoma heat, and not even finding a trace of these cows, I was done. I felt like I was just going in circles and finding nothing. I was ready to call it quits and head to the house. Finally, David said, let's go back and grab some lunch and

DAY - WORKING WITH DAVID

we'll try and figure out what to do next. As we rode up to the corrals, much to our surprise and joy, there they were – two mommas and a baby. But as soon as they got a look at us their heads went up and the chase was on. We ended up roping all three and got them all safely in the corrals! Boy did it feel good to find them and catch them after such a long day!

As I reflect back on that day, I'm reminded that sometimes every day feels the same. You may think things like, "I can't say anything right to my spouse", or "my day at work stunk!" Something *breaks* and you find yourselves hopeless and wanting to quit. But then you get that *break—y*our day at work gets better because your boss comes in and says something encouraging, your spouse wraps their arms around you and you feel loved—and that changes your whole attitude. This is what God does when we trust in Him and wait for His provision. Life is going to stink sometimes, but if we seek God in the midst of it all, he will, as today's verse says, "put a new song in my mouth" and our pity turns to praise!

CHEW ON THIS

In what area of your life do you find yourself hopeless? Do you have the faith to keep on seeking God even when life stinks? Do you need to take a look back at your life and remember what God has done for you and how he

TIED ON

has put a new song in your mouth? When was the last time you praised Him for all the goodness he has shown you?

PRAYER

God, thank you for all you do for me. Though I may feel hopeless, you want to put a new song in my mouth! I praise you for your goodness! It's in your holy name I pray, Amen.

WEEK 15

DON'T LET DEATH LOSS DEFINE YOUR HERD

PHILIPPIANS 4:8
Finally, brothers and sisters, whatever is true, whatever is noble, whatever is right, whatever is pure, whatever is lovely, whatever is admirable—if anything is excellent or praiseworthy—think about such things.

If you're in the cattle business, then you know that sometimes cattle die. While death loss is inevitable, what I've learned is that I can't let death loss define my herd. If I lose a calf or cow, I have to choose to remain focused on the herd that I still have and not let the death loss determine my success.

Similar to the rancher with death loss, we all face

loss and hard times. But, there are some things we can do to prevent us from being defined by the losses of life. First off, we must allow God to change our perspective—just like a rancher who can't stay focused on the ones that died but has to focus on the herd that is still alive, we must also search for the good things in our lives and choose to focus on those things. God's Word tells us to keep our minds focused on the things that are *right, lovely, and praiseworthy*. You may be thinking, "Nothing is going right in my life," but, there is always something that we can praise God for. By doing this, our attitude will be different even when we face the dark days of life!

We must also practice following God's principles. God's Word can minimize poor decisions and failures. Psalm 119:105 says, "Your word is a lamp for my feet, a light on my path." When we let the light of God's Truth fill our minds and show us what paths we should take, we tend to face less self-inflicted dark days!

CHEW ON THIS
In what ways have you let your dark days define you? Are you more focused on your failings or what God says is true about you? Is your mind focused on things that are right, lovely and praiseworthy?

DON'T LET DEATH LOSS DEFINE YOUR HERD

PRAYER

God, help me to do my part in preventing the dark days in my life. Show me your paths for my life. Help me not become consumed by the hard times but to focus on you. It's in your holy name I pray, Amen.

WEEK 16

DON'T RUN 'EM TOO FAR

JEREMIAH 17:14
Heal me, LORD, and I will be healed; save me and I will be saved, for you are the one I praise.

It was the fall of 2012 and I was in Hutchison, Kansas, day-working for my friends Josh and Caleb Nine. We were doctoring yearlings on some corn stock circles. After caking the calves, we rode through them to see if we could find any sick calves that might need doctoring. After finding a calf that was most definitely not feeling good, we sorted him off and Caleb told me to rope him. Before I started toward the calf, he said something that I'll never forget: "Don't run 'em too far, he's sick." After catching the calf and successfully getting it doctored, I was reminded

DON'T RUN 'EM TOO FAR

of his words and it got me to thinking.

There are a few things I've learned when doctoring calves: 1) A good cowboy doesn't run the calf too far. The ideal scenario is to get to the calf quickly and get him roped with as little stress as possible; 2) Even though the cowboy is trying to save the calf's life, almost every calf runs; and 3) The medicine the cowboy provides helps heal sickness and keep the animal alive.

Spiritually speaking, the cowboy in this story represents Jesus Christ who wants to provide for us what is essential for living a godly life. The calf represents me and you—sin-sick sinners in need of forgiveness and healing. But like the calf that always runs, we too most often run from God. Why do we run? It may be because of our sin. It may be because we don't feel worthy of God's healing provision. But either way the cool thing about God is that even when we run, he chases after us with the desire to give us the proper meds that we need to find healing. We would be smarter than that calf if we would not run and just turn to Him, confess our sin, get honest with Him, and find forgiveness and grace.

CHEW ON THIS

Do you find yourself running from God today? If so, stop. Turn back to Him and find his healing grace. None of us deserve it, but He offers it anyway!

TIED ON

PRAYER

God, thank you for your mercy and grace. Thank you for loving me even though I don't deserve it. Please help me to show others grace and mercy as you have to me. It's in your holy name I pray, Amen.

WEEK 17

END OF THE ROPE

PHILIPPIANS 4:19
And my God will meet all your needs according to his glorious riches in Christ Jesus.

Years ago when Heather and I were dating, I had my own place in town, but had the urge to get back into owning and starting a few horses. So, because Heather's grandpa raised horses, we decided to bring home a few yearlings to start. I had about an acre or so of land but no corrals, round pen, or even any panels. Needless to say, even though I had left the halters on them so they could drag the lead rope, as I let them loose in the pasture, I thought to myself, *once I let these yearlings go, how the crap am I going to catch them?* A few days later I decided that it was time to start working with them. As you can imagine, that was easier said than done. I chased them around on foot until I was about to need EMS to come bring me some

TIED ON

oxygen. Finally I went and got a rope and for another 30 minutes tried to get them cornered so I could rope them Finally I got one caught and that's when the race started.

This filly got her head turned away from me and I wasn't able to do much to stop her. As I tried to hold her, the rope burned through my hands and at that moment I had a sinking feeling that the neighbors were watching me and thinking, "What a greenhorn." As I hit the knot at the end of the rope, I was running at that speed when you know you are going way too fast for a human to be going. I just knew that I was going to do that trip-and-roll-while-sliding-on-the-ground flip. By the grace of God I didn't trip, but I did lose the rope, and it was at that point that I decided to let her drag the rope around for a few days, because one of us was fixing to die—her from a bullet or me from lack of oxygen.

In life there are also times where we've roped something that's way out of our control. It may be a relationship that you are trying desperately to hold onto, an illness that is beyond your control, your job, or your kids, but whatever it is, you find yourself at the end of the rope going way too fast! What the heck are we to do when we find ourselves in this situation? Well, Elijah, who was a chosen man of God, had gone through some pretty trying events. He fought many battles, his life was threatened, he was on the run, and he felt afraid, depressed,

END OF THE ROPE

and abandoned. He was at the end of his rope and he wanted to die. On top of all of that, God tells Elijah that there's going to be a drought and this drought would last for three years. But even though Elijah felt hopeless and out of control, God provided help where and when Elijah least expected it. God provided a brook for Elijah to drink from during the drought, and he was fed from the ravines. Talk about unexpected! But the truth is, that's exactly how God works sometimes. When we feel like we are at the end our rope, God is there to provide. Just when you find yourself at the end of the rope—just when life's at that speed of being way out of control—God can and will provide. All we have to do is trust Him.

CHEW ON THIS

Are you at the end of your rope? What events in your life have you running out of control? What provision are you needing from God today?

PRAYER

Lord, help me to trust you when I'm at the end of the rope. You tell me you will meet all of my needs, help me to rest in that promise. It's in your holy name I pray, Amen.

TIED ON

WEEK 18

FORWARD MOTION

ECCLESIASTES 4:9-10
Two are better than one, because they have a good return for their labor: If either of them falls down, one can help the other up. But pity anyone who falls and has no one to help them up.

In my experience with starting colts, one major key to getting through a sticky spot is "forward motion." If you can get the colt to move his feet, training them is so much easier. However, there are many times when you've done your work under saddle and then you saddle a colt, throw your leg over to make that first ride and the colt will refuse to move out. One of the methods I've used that works well in this situation, is to have someone on

FORWARD MOTION

the ground in the round pen helping you get the horse to move forward. This person may use a flag or a rope to get the colt to move its feet. With both the rider and the person on the ground working together, it usually takes less energy, not to mention if the colt gets the best of you, and you get bucked off, you will have someone there to take you to the hospital (chuckle, chuckle).

The same is true for us, as Christians. We are all going to experience some sticky spots in life. You lose your job, your marriage lacks passion, or your spiritual walk is dull and struggling. These are all sticky spots in life where, if you have someone there to help and encourage you to move forward in Christ, it makes it a lot easier. As today's verse tell us, *two are better than one*, and if we stick together, and try not to get through life's sticky spots alone, we will have a better chance of succeeding in life and bringing God glory. That said, while our earthly friends can be a godsend, Jesus is our ultimate friend, and it's His friendship that we should lean on most when we feel stuck.

CHEW ON THIS
What sticky spot do you find yourself in today that you need a friend's help to get you out? Are you trying to go through the storms of life alone? Have you turned to God to help you move forward?

TIED ON

PRAYER

Lord, help me to not try to go through the storms of life alone. Thank you for sending me people to do life with and to help me get into forward motion. Help me to be a friend to someone in a sticky spot right now. It's in your holy name I pray, Amen.

WEEK 19

FROM THE PIT TO THE PLATFORM

ROMANS 8:28
And we know that in all things God works for the good of those who love him, who have been called according to his purpose.

Mary Walker joined the Women's Pro Rodeo Association in 1983. As a barrel racer of almost thirty years, there had been some ups and downs but none worse than the events of 2011. That year she lost her son in an auto accident at the age of twenty-one. A couple months later, Walker suffered the worst injury of her long career. While riding her new bay horse, Latte, the horse slipped going around the final barrel at a rodeo and fell on Mary. Walker broke her pelvis, her hip in three places, two vertebrae, and a pair of toes. Because of this accident, she faced a

TIED ON

long and daunting rehabilitation process. In just a two-month period, both her heart and body had been broken and she found herself at the lowest point of her life.

Rather than lie down and just give up her dream of being a world champion barrel racer, Walker chose to fight and work to heal both her heart and body. After months of rehab, the doctors told her she was fixed and the only thing that would stop her would be what was between her ears! That very next year, Mary set a new WPRA record for earnings by winning over $146,000, and her horse, Latte, was named barrel horse of the year! And at the age of fifty-three, she not only qualified for her first WNFR, but at the end of the world finals, she found herself on the platform receiving her first world championship buckle. Her story is one of someone who went from the pit to the platform.

Maybe you find yourself at your lowest today. Maybe you've experienced a devastating loss and your heart is broken. Maybe you've just received a diagnosis that you have a terminal illness. My prayer is that like Mary, you will pick yourself up off the ground, allow God to heal your wounds, and get back in the game! Truth is, as long as we remain faithful to loving Him, especially in the pits of life, He will work all things for our good and His glory!

FROM THE PIT TO THE PLATFORM

CHEW ON THIS
What pit do you find yourself in today? Have you given up hope or are you allowing God to pick up your broken life and get back in the saddle? Turn to him. Remain faithful to Him and he will lift you up!

PRAYER
God, thank you for always being with me, even in the pit. Thank you that there is no place I can go that is away from you. Please help me to trust in you and your faithfulness to pull me through and out of the pit. It's in your holy name I pray, Amen.

TIED ON

WEEK 20

GIVING CREDIT WHERE CREDIT IS DUE

PROVERBS 3:6
In all your ways acknowledge him . . .

I've got some pretty safe, dependable, bombproof horses. How did I get them that way? I used methods that I learned from some of the best horse trainers in the world. From desensitizing, to learning that miles and wet saddle blankets are the key to training a safe horse, I learned it all from them. When people ask me how I got that done with my horse, I try to always give credit to those who taught me. I wouldn't be worth my weight as a colt starter if I didn't have these guys teaching me these methods.

As believers, acknowledging Him (Christ) in all we do is one of the greatest acts of obedience that we can do!

GIVING CREDIT WHERE CREDIT IS DUE

What does this look like? It means that we give Him credit for every area of our lives! From our job, to our truck, horses, homes, and kids, we are to give Him all the credit for these things (and give Him control of them as well).

People will ask, "How did you get so lucky?" Our reply should be, "It's not luck, it's all because of the grace of God. Everything I have is because of Him."

The truth is, as Christians, we should not be ashamed of the God who gives us life, joy, peace, and love! We should willingly share why we are so blessed with anyone, anywhere. Is this always easy? No, but it is always right! We must trust in the Lord with all our heart, lean not on our own understanding, and in all our ways acknowledge Him.

CHEW ON THIS

When was the last time you gave credit to God in public? Do you realize all you have is because of the grace of God? How can you acknowledge Him at work and at home?

PRAYER

Lord, forgive me where I have not acknowledged you for all you've done in my life. Help me open my mouth and give you all the glory for what you've done for me so that others can be drawn to you. It's in your holy name I pray, Amen.

TIED ON

WEEK 21

GREEDY COWBOY

COLOSSIANS 3:5
Put to death, therefore, whatever belongs to your earthly [sinful] nature: sexual immorality, impurity, lust, evil desires and greed, which is idolatry.

One of the things that God has blessed me with, is the ability to take pictures of the working cowboys that I get to ride with on the great ranches of Northwest Oklahoma and West Texas. I've even had a few of my pictures make the cover of some great western magazines. The other day I got a call from the editor for *Working Ranch Magazine.* He wanted to put one of my pictures on the cover of their magazine. As we were talking he threw out a price that he would pay for my picture and asked me if the amount

GREEDY COWBOY

would work. At that moment God revealed to me a flaw in my character. I discovered what being greedy felt like. See, when he asked if that price would work, I thought for just a split second, *no it won't work, I want more!* Instead of being honored and feeling privileged to be on the cover a magazine that goes out to 55,000 ranchers all across the country, and having my picture don the cover of a magazine in every Tractor Supply store, I wanted more!

The truth is, we are all greedy in one way or another. We want to keep the best for ourselves. We want to always get the better end of the deal and not worry about the other guy. But as Christ followers, we are called to put greed to death. So, the question we should be asking is: *How do we overcome being greedy?* A couple ways to overcome greed are to be grateful and generous. We should possess a grateful attitude, knowing that all we have comes from the Lord. We must be generous, realizing that what we have was given to us by God and that God desires for us to use what we have to bless others. Do you have a nice truck? Then enjoy your nice truck, trailer, or horse, but use them to bless others as well! Do you have a great home? Enjoy your home, but open it up to be a blessing to someone else. By asking God to help you be grateful for what you have and practice generosity, you will be able to overcome the greed in your life!

TIED ON

CHEW ON THIS

How greedy are you? Are you grateful for everything the Lord has given you? Do you thank Him daily for the stuff you have? How generous are you with your stuff? Ask God to help you be more grateful and generous with the things He has given you and watch how He uses you to bless others.

PRAYER

Lord, help me not to be greedy. Help me to remember that everything I has is a gift from You. I want to use what I've been given to be a blessing to others. Show me how I can do that more. It's in Your holy name I pray, Amen.

WEEK 22

HAPPY TRIALS

JAMES 1:12
Blessed is the one who perseveres under trial, because when he has stood the test, he will receive the crown of life that God has promised to those who love him.

We've all heard the great cowboy song, "Happy Trails" right? Well, after a long day of working cattle and some not so happy events, I renamed this song, "Happy Trials". If you've ever worked with cattle you know it can be very trying. In just one day I was kicked by a heifer and knocked to the ground, had fallen off the platform of the cattle tub, and knocked the crap out of my elbow on the working chute. To top it off, I had this one cowboy yelling at me all day, 'cause for some reason he thought he was in charge. I wanted to break his nose (in Jesus name of course)! Needless to say, I wasn't a very happy person that day and it was one day I wished I never had to face.

TIED ON

Trials are inevitable. The world's definition of happiness is the absence of trials, heartache, persecution, pain, death, and loss. And because of all of these trials, many people aren't happy! Depression diagnoses are at the highest they've ever been. There's suicide, divorce, and abandonment, all of which are high because people don't know how to deal with the trials of life.

In today's verse, the word "blessed" literally means *happy*, but not in the sense that the world views happiness. The Lord's definition of "blessed" or "happiness" is not the absence of trials, but the victory over them.

If by the Lord's strength we will endure and choose to face our trials with Him, we will overcome! We can't get rid of trials, but we can find victory over them.

Philippians 4:13 tells us, "I can do all things through Christ who strengthens me."

CHEW ON THIS
Have you allowed your trials to steal your happiness? Are you living for the world's definition of happiness or God's?

PRAYER
Lord, help me find victory over my trials through you. Heal my pain and comfort me through the trials of life so that I can overcome! It's in your holy name I pray, Amen.

WEEK 23

HAVE YOU BEEN CASTRATED?

1 CORINTHIANS 16:13-14
Be watchful, stand firm in the faith, act like men, be strong. Let all that you do be done in love. (ESV)

One of the most important jobs while working calves is cutting them. Some citified people may think that this practice is cruel, but they think *wrong*. Castration is considered to be a necessary management practice for cattle. It reduces the aggressiveness of the calf by lowering the testosterone levels, therefore making it safer for the calf and the cattle owner. Also, steers (castrated calves) tend to have a higher quality grade of meat—are more consistent, have better marbling, and tender beef. Steers also tend to bring more than bulls at the sale. So what are the disadvantages? The answer's obvious—they can't reproduce! They will live and die without the ability to raise anything but themselves.

Sadly, for years we've seen the castration of men from the church. This is a major reason why many churches are not reproducing, but rather dying out. One reason why men have been castrated from the church is that a lot of men fear having to give up their manhood to love Jesus. Because a lot of churches look, feel, and act more feminine, a lot of men *steer* clear of going *(pun intended)*. But as we see in today's verse, being a godly man doesn't mean that you have to give up your manhood. If anything godly men are called by God to be masculine. Paul says, "act like men."

Because of what we see on TV and in the media, many men have become castrated cowards! I'm sick of this lack of men being men, and I'm going to do my best to empower, encourage, and engage men to be the Godly masculine men that God has asked them to be! In a world that downplays and even discourages men from acting like men, I believe God desires for men of God to be different. I believe that God has called men to display bravery in the site of danger, courage in the midst of the fight, heroism in the midst of cowards, and intestinal fortitude in the site of injustice! In order for men to return to the church, we must allow men to be what God created them to be: Godly and masculine!

HAVE YOU BEEN CASTRATED?

CHEW ON THIS

Are you a Godly man? Are you living out your God-given masculinity? Are you courageous, strong, and brave when called for? Do your sons and daughters respect you or are you just a passive pushover? The church and the world need men to act like men for the glory of God and the good of others!

PRAYER

God, thank you that I am called to "act like a man". Please show me what that looks like for me and help me to fulfill my role as a godly masculine man. Use me to help grow the church through inviting my friends and showing them that they can love You and still be a man! It's in your holy name I pray, Amen.

WEEK 24

HESITATING GETS YOU HURT

MATTHEW 14:26-29

When the disciples saw him walking on the lake, they were terrified. "It's a ghost," they said, and cried out in fear. But Jesus immediately said to them: "Take courage! It is I. Don't be afraid!" "Lord, if it is you," Peter replied, "tell me to come to you on the water." "Come", he said. Then Peter got down out of the boat, walked on the water and came to Jesus.

How many of you have ever hesitated a second too long and you paid the price for it?

When it comes to cowboyin', you cannot hesitate! In a ranch rodeo, if you hesitate when you're going to milk a wild cow, you might give her just enough time to swing around and mow you over! If you hesitate when cornering a four-weight calf on the ground, you might get your

HESITATING GETS YOU HURT

teeth kicked in! If you hesitate while throwing your leg over a green two-year-old, you might get yard darted! The point is, you can't hesitate!

Spiritually speaking, we must not hesitate! I'm sure you have been in situations where you found yourself in a bad way. You may have found out some bad news, experienced loss, or maybe a storm of pain or disappointment blew into your life and you found yourself full of fear.

In the story from today's Scripture, we see how the disciples were in a bad way. The storm is raging and there is what seems to be like a ghost walking on the water. The disciples are terrified! But, Jesus *immediately* tells them not to be afraid. Jesus knew they were scared and that he needed to give them peace! So Jesus didn't hesitate. We also see that Peter didn't hesitate either! We see him get out of the boat and trust Jesus enough to walk on water! Jesus told him to "come" and he came. What about you? Maybe Jesus has told you to come, but you've hesitated? Maybe He's told you to do something for years, but you've said "*Nah.*" Maybe He's told you to forgive someone, or most importantly maybe Jesus has been asking you to give your heart to Him—don't hesitate. Get to it!

CHEW ON THIS

Has Jesus told you to do something but you're hesitating? Are you in the middle of a storm in life and God has told

TIED ON

you to take action, but you're hesitating? What is it going to take for you to get out of the boat and obey?

PRAYER
Lord, help me not to hesitate when you ask me to do something. Increase my faith and trust in you so I can respond without hesitation! It's in your holy name I pray, Amen.

WEEK 25

HIS ANIMALS COME FIRST

MATTHEW 6:33
But seek first his kingdom and his righteousness, and all these things will be given to you as well.

A long-time code that most cowboys live by, is that your animals always come first. It doesn't matter if it's really hot, really windy, or freezing outside, a cowboy's first priority is making sure the cows and horses are cared for before his/her day is done. This code is followed even if that means a longer day, less sleep, or freezing to death.

Like a cowboy, as Christians we are called to make Christ #1 in our lives. What does that look like? To put Christ first means that His will, His glory, and His pleasure becomes our #1 priority. This commitment to putting

TIED ON

Him first may come at the expense of our own comfort, goals, and happiness. But Jesus promises us as believers that if we put Him first, we will be blessed beyond our wildest dreams and find fulfillment like we've never felt. The only prerequisite is we must put Him first.

If you're anything like me, you get your priorities out of whack sometimes. Maybe you've become a workaholic and your family feels neglected. Maybe your priority in life has been to own a bunch of stuff, and you've sacrificed what God really wanted you to do with your money for your own pleasure. Maybe you've put more weight in finding the right relationship, therefore causing your relationship with God to become second. Sadly, when these things take the place of God, we find ourselves unsatisfied even when we end up getting what we had replaced God with. But, if we will put Christ first, and keep Him first, we will ultimately find true joy and happiness.

CHEW ON THIS
Are you seeking things of this world more than the things of God? If you were to list your priorities what would be at the top? How can you assure that Christ stays #1 in your life?

HIS ANIMALS COME FIRST

PRAYER

Lord, I want to make loving and serving you my #1 priority. Help me to seek you first in every area of my life. It's in your holy name I pray, Amen.

WEEK 26

HURRY UP AND WAIT

PSALM 27:14
Wait for the Lord; be strong and take heart and wait for the Lord.

From the outside looking in, people might think I'm a patient man, but get me in the round pen with a two-year-old colt or ask me to help gather cattle, and you will find out pretty quickly that I'm not that patient. Instead of waiting for the correct response from my colt, I want to force it. Instead of waiting on those cows to choose to go, in I want to make them go in. But the more I've worked with horses and cattle, the more the phrase, "hurry up and wait," proves true. When you wait on a horse to give you the correct response, the horse learns and you get

HURRY UP AND WAIT

along better. When you wait on one cow to be a leader and lead the others into the pen, it usually works better than forcing them.

The same is true when it comes to waiting on the Lord. Many times we don't wait on the Lord because we think we can get it done quicker or more easily our way. Well, that same phrase that pays when working with cattle or horses works in our spiritual lives also—*hurry up and wait*. Instead of trying to make something happen ourselves, we are to wait on the Lord! We are to wait on His answers to our questions about life. We are to wait for Him to show us what His will is or His plans are!

David, the writer of the Psalms, figured out that waiting on the Lord pays in the end: Psalm 40:1-3:

> I waited patiently for the Lord; he turned to me and heard my cry. He lifted me up out of the slimy pit, out of the mud and mire; he set my feet on a rock and gave me a firm place to stand. He put a new song in my mouth, a hymn of praise to our God. Many will see and fear and put their trust in the Lord.

David was in many pits! He committed adultery with Bathsheba. He murdered. He did things his way, instead of waiting on God's provision. But finally, because he waited

TIED ON

patiently on the Lord, the Lord lifted him out of the pit!

CHEW ON THIS
What decision are you making on your own right now that you should be waiting on God's answer before moving forward?

PRAYER
God, help me to be strong as I wait for you. Help me to trust that you will work everything out for your glory if I will just wait for your perfect timing. In Jesus name I pray, Amen.

WEEK 27

I'M YOUR HUCKLEBERRY

JOHN 15:12-14

My command is this: Love each other as I have loved you. Greater love has no one than this, that he lay down his life for his friends. You are my friends if you do what I command.

The movie *Tombstone* tells the story about the famous Earp brothers and their reign as lawmen in the town of Tombstone. Although the movie is more about Wyatt and his brothers, my favorite character is "Doc Holliday" played by Val Kilmer. Both in real life and in the movie, Wyatt and Doc Holliday had a special admiration and love for one another. They had fun playing cards together, but also fought a lot of outlaws together. The proof of their loyalty to one another is found in one of the most

TIED ON

famous scenes in western film history. Johnny Ringo, the second-in-command of the outlaw gang *The Cowboys*, and known as the fastest gunslinger in the west, challenges Wyatt Earp to a duel. But before the duel, Wyatt goes and sees Doc Holliday who, because of his hard living of smoking and drinking, is bed ridden and seems to be on his last leg. As the scene plays on, Wyatt leaves to go face Johnny Ringo, and we see that Doc isn't as sick as he led Wyatt to believe and he makes his way over to the duel with Johnny Ringo before Wyatt does. So, when Doc shows up, Ringo, isn't able to tell that it isn't Wyatt and says, "I didn't think you had it in ya." Doc replies with some famous words, "I'm your huckleberry." Johnny Ringo tries to back out, but then suddenly gets the nerve to pull his gun, but Doc is too quick and shoots him right between the eyes and kills him dead. Wyatt shows up seconds later, seeing Johnny Ringo lying on the ground dead and realizes that Doc had more than likely-saved his life!

After watching that scene, I began to ask the question: *what does it mean to be somebody's huckleberry?* Well, by saying this to Johnny Ringo, he is basically saying, "I'm the man that's going to get this job done." What I realized from Wyatt and Doc's friendship was that by Doc stepping in and taking Wyatt's place in the duel, Doc was showing his love by fighting Wyatt's battle.

I'M YOUR HUCKLEBERRY

I believe that that's exactly what God does for us. When we face battles with the enemy Jesus shows up and says to the enemy, *"I'm your huckleberry. You want a fight? Let's do it!"* and he defeats Satan, the Johnny Ringo of this world. Doc showed Wyatt what a true friendship looks like, by being willing to lay down his life for his friend if needed. Jesus took it a step further, by actually laying down His life and dying so that sin and Satan might be defeated. I praise God for Jesus' example to us and I pray that when the battle comes, that we would be willing to fight for our fellow brothers and sisters even to the point of laying down our lives for one another.

CHEW ON THIS
What battles do you see a friend or a family member fixing to have to fight that you can step in and fight the battle for them? What does it look like for you to love sacrificially and selflessly?

PRAYER
Lord, thank you for being my huckleberry! Help me to lay down my life for others and love like you do. It's in your holy name I pray, Amen.

WEEK 28

JAKE AND JUDAS

JOHN 12:4-6

But one of his disciples, Judas Iscariot, who was later to betray him, objected. "Why wasn't this perfume sold and the money given to the poor? It was worth a year's wages." He did not say this because he cared about the poor but because he was a thief; as keeper of the money bag, he used to help himself to what was put into it.

In the TV miniseries *Lonesome Dove,* we find some of TV's greatest western characters—Gus, Captain Call, Pee and Deets to name a few. But the one character that we all pity and even hate for the way he acted was Jake Spoon. Jake, like Gus and Captain Call, was a former Texas Ranger, though he ends up a fugitive on the run after accidentally shooting a dentist in a bar fight. After returning to Lonesome Dove, Jake was the one who came up with the idea to drive cattle from Texas to Montana

JAKE AND JUDAS

and start the first cattle ranch there. Gus and Captain Call decided they would go, but Jake backed out and decided to go his own way. Later in the movie, we see that Jake joins up with a group of horse thieves who end up being cold-blooded murderers. After Gus and Woodrow come up on some of the murdered and innocent victims, they decide to hunt down the killers and see justice served. After tracking them and finally catching up to them, they find Jake riding with these outlaws. Jake tries to convince them that he didn't do anything wrong, but Woodrow and Gus decide that by riding with these murderers, Jake is just as guilty. They tell Jake, "You ride with an outlaw, you die with an outlaw!"

In the Bible, we find another character that had every opportunity to do good. He had good friends, walked amongst Jesus, and was taught what was right and wrong. But instead of following these teachings, he chose to betray rather than believe. His name: Judas Iscariot.

While Jake was a Texas Ranger (and he's obviously a fictional character) I believe his personal character had always been somewhat rotten. While on the outside he was charming and appeared to be a man of integrity, he was really bent toward evil. The same can be said about Judas. We could argue whether Judas was a believer or not, but one thing was for certain—he was a fake. Judas' betrayal of Jesus was not a change in his character—it

TIED ON

was a revealing of his character. He hadn't changed; he had simply been exposed.

What does this mean for us as Christians? First we must strive to be authentic Christians who not only talk the talk, but walk the walk. We must prove our faith by spending one on one time with Him daily. We must know Him, not just believe in Him. We must worship Him, not just sing songs. We must love Him, not just give Him lip service. So the question is: *Are you a fake or are you a true follower?* I pray you are a true follower.

CHEW ON THIS

Are you the same person in private that you are in public? Do you have a personal growing relationship with Christ, or are you a fake?

PRAYER

Lord, help me to be the same in private that I am in public. Help me not to live a fake life, but a life that is genuinely in love with you. It's in your holy name I pray, Amen.

WEEK 29

LEARNING FROM BETTER HORSEMEN

PROVERBS 3:5
... and lean not on your own understanding.

I'm to the point now in my horsemanship where I want to go to the next level! I want to advance my horses to be able to perform better. The problem is, I don't have the knowledge to take them there. Because of this, I'm learning that I need to seek out guys that are better horseman than me and find the knowledge to take my horses further! If I don't, my horses will probably digress rather than progress to the next level!

The same is true for us as Christians. When we try to do things in our own limited wisdom, we can only go so far. When we start thinking that we know what's best for our lives, and we stop trusting in God, we get into some

TIED ON

deep trouble!

Proverbs 14:12 says, "There is a way that seems right to a man, but in the end it leads to death." God is not saying to turn your brains off and become mindless robots. We are to use our intellect and common sense, but not depend on them alone. We must turn to God for more wisdom and rely on His understanding. We should pray and ask for wisdom in every aspect of life!

Listen to James 1:5, "If any of you lacks wisdom, he should ask God, who gives generously to all without finding fault, and it will be given to him." This verse shows us that if we need more wisdom all we have to do is ask! We need to quit trying to lean on our own limited understanding of life, and seek the One with unlimited knowledge and understanding!

CHEW ON THIS

Do you try to do things in your own wisdom? Do you try to rely on your own understanding? What decisions are you facing right now that you need to ask God for more wisdom? Ask Him to help you seek His wisdom for every area of your life!

PRAYER

Lord, forgive me where I have tried to do things on my own.

LEARNING FROM BETTER HORSEMEN

Give me wisdom that can only come from you. Thank you for giving your wisdom generously to us when we ask. It's in your holy name I pray, Amen.

WEEK 30

LONG LIVE COWBOYS

HEBREWS 13:8
Jesus Christ is the same yesterday and today and forever.

We live in a world that is constantly changing. From the engines in our trucks, to the weather, to the way we dress, even to the phones we carry, everything is always changing. While I embrace a lot of these changes, when it comes to the life we live as cowboys and ranchers, I like for some things to stay the same. From riding horses instead of 4 wheelers, dragging calves to the fire instead of using a calf table, to building a wood fire instead of a branding pot, I want these things to never change. Some people would see these practices as out of date or unnecessary with all the technological advances of modern day, and while I agree that many of the changes in the ranching world have made life easier, I love it when I see the same things that have been done for years still being done today!

In a world that is changing around us by the minute, there is one thing, or should I say person, that never changes and his name is Jesus. Today's verse tells us that He is *the same yesterday, today, and forever*! Unfortunately, some people hear this verse and think, "That proves it. Jesus is out of touch and out of date with today's culture." But that would be far from the truth. This verse isn't saying that Jesus doesn't recognize the world we live in. The fact is, He knows what's going to happen next before we do! He makes changes to the world and our lives constantly. What doesn't change though, is His love for you and me! We never have to worry that He will someday stop loving us. Jesus Christ loves us today as much as He did the day He walked up that hill carrying the cross, and was crucified for you and for me. His love is the same yesterday, today, and forever, and for that I'm very thankful.

CHEW ON THIS

Do you sometimes wonder if Jesus has stopped caring about you? Do you fear that you may lose His love because of something you've done? We can be solid, obedient followers, or be the sorriest, good-for-nothing person that sins every minute, but His love for us is just the same. His

TIED ON

love for us never changes. Thank Him for that today!

PRAYER

God, thank you for being the same yesterday, today, and forever. Thank you that I never have to worry about losing your love. Please help me rest in that truth and in you. It's in your holy name I pray, Amen.

WEEK 31

MORE HORSE

EPHESIANS 3:20
Now to him who is able to do immeasurably more than all we ask or imagine...

The other day, I sold two of my horses that I not only started myself, but had used as ranch horses for years, and here's the reason why—I want more *horse*. Sure the horses I sold were dependable sticks and did their jobs well, but they couldn't deliver the skills that you only find in a great horse! I've never truly ridden a great horse and I would not only love to ride one, but I would love to own one! And so I want more horse. Maybe you're a rodeo cowboy or a barrel racer, and you can't get enough. Every rodeo you go to leaves you wanting more. I feel ya! People ask me what I do for fun and I say, "I cowboy for fun". I can't get enough of it! If I weren't a preacher, I would be on horseback every day! Every day I'm out there work-

TIED ON

ing, leaves me wanting more!

We all want more of the things we love—but I believe that as followers in Jesus Christ, we should want more of Him. You may be thinking, "What do you mean by that?" I believe we ought to pray bold prayers like, "Bring it on Lord, give me more!" I want more of you! I want more of your joy! I want more of your peace! I want to please you more! I want to serve you more! I want to love you more! The cool thing about God is that when we ask for more, He can always deliver. I want you to hear this. God can give you more. All He asks you to do is trust Him and ask Him for more.

CHEW ON THIS

Do you want more faith? Do you want more power? Do you want more fun? Ask the Lord who is able to give you *immeasurably more than all we ask or imagine.*

PRAYER

Lord, I thank you that no matter how much we ask from you, you can give more. And so, Lord, I thank you for that. I praise you for what you've already done in my life and I pray that you would give me more of your spirit, more of your love, and more of your strength. It's in your holy name I pray, Amen.

WEEK 32

NO NEED FOR A NIGHT LATCH

PROVERBS 3:5-6
Trust in the Lord with all your heart, and lean not on your own understanding; in all your ways acknowledge him, and he will make your paths straight.

If you've ever tried to get a job done on a horse you didn't trust, you know it's not much fun. You ride with your butt puckered and your hand in the night latch because you know he's going to blow up, you just don't know when! I've been there and it's not very fun.

On the other hand, if you've ever had a horse you *can* trust when it's time to get a job done, you know how good that feels! You can saddle him up after he's been out to pasture for awhile and just trot off like you've been ridin' him all week! You feel safe and you trust him to take care of you whether you're racin' across a wheat pasture doctorin' a sick yearling or going head to head with a mad momma cow!

Spiritually speaking, the great thing about God is that He is trustworthy! We can trust Him no matter the task, no matter the obstacle and no matter what crazy circumstance we've got.

Romans 8:28 says, "And we know that in all things God works for the good of those who love him, who have been called according to his purpose." If we love and trust the Lord, He can work out everything for our good! God wants to be a part of every decision we make, great or small. But the bigger the decision, the more we better trust in God! The harder the task, the more trust we have to have!

CHEW ON THIS

Some of you have made some major decisions without trusting God before making them, and you've paid the price! You didn't trust that Christ would see you through and you took a wrong turn! And now you've got yourself in a bind!

You might be wondering what to do. You need to turn from your sin, confess what you did wrong and trust in

NO NEED FOR A NIGHT LATCH

God! Trusting in God is the only way to go!

PRAYER
Lord, forgive me where I haven't trusted you with my life. Help me to trust you even when I don't understand what you're doing. Make my paths straight. It's in your holy name I pray, Amen.

WEEK 33

PREPARED TO DRAG

PSALM 37:7
Be still before the Lord and wait patiently on him...

Spring is one of my favorite times of the year! Why? Because it's brandin' season! Many ranchers and cowboys get together to help each other brand, vaccinate, and work their calves. If you're like me and you don't get to cowboy for a living and you're waiting for the first day of branding season, it's a good idea to get prepared. A good cowboy will make sure their gear is in working order. They'll get their horse legged up, trimmed, and ready for the coming season. Then when the call comes to go day-work, they are ready!

As Christians, we are also called to wait on the Lord.

PREPARED TO DRAG

However, like the day-worker, we are called to prepare for God's call to go to work even while we wait. When we are waiting on God for an answer to prayer, direction for a job, or to show us our next task, we should be using our time to read His Word, pray, and serve Him. Psalm 27:14 says, "Wait for the Lord; be strong and take heart and wait for the Lord." How do we get strong spiritually? We exercise our faith even while we wait. We wait patiently, but we don't just sit idle. We don't just wait on God to do everything—we have to do our part! We have to continually prepare ourselves for His call!

CHEW ON THIS
Are you prepared for what He is going to do, or are you sitting idle and expecting Him to do all the work? Ask God to show you what he wants you to do while you wait on His answer or direction, and get after it!

PRAYER
Lord, help me to seek you. Help me to live for you while I wait for you. Help me to be still before you so that I can hear you when you're ready to move in my life! In Jesus name I pray, Amen.

WEEK 34

RIDING SHOTGUN

1 CORINTHIANS 16:13
Be on your guard; stand firm in your faith; be men of courage; be strong.

In old western movies, when trouble came and you had to get away from the bad guys, the stagecoach driver was the one that kept the wagon moving so not to give the bad guys an easier way to get control of the wagon. But there was another guy up front that carried a shotgun and would use it to protect the driver and passengers from the would-be attackers. This is where we get the famous phrase, "riding shotgun."

From today's Scripture, one could say that the stagecoach driver is God, and He is calling us to ride shotgun.

RIDING SHOTGUN

The verse tells us to "be on our guard" and spot the dangers that could destroy us and our precious cargo (which in most cases, would be our family). We are called to guard our families from the devil and his evil schemes! How do we do this? We are to pray, love, and protect our spouse and our kids. We are told to be courageous, to be strong, and stand firm when the enemy attacks. We are to build our family up through providing words of encouragement and acts of kindness so that when temptation rears its ugly head, they aren't lacking these things and fall to temptation. We need to fill our kids' minds with the truth of Scripture so that they can stand firm in the face of an attack. We need to take advantage of every opportunity to show them how to fight spiritual battles with the supernatural weapons of God.

Satan would love nothing more than to destroy us and our families. This is why we as husbands and wives and fathers and mothers need to ride shotgun—always on guard, standing firm in our faith and being courageous!

CHEW ON THIS
What ways are you riding shotgun for your family? What areas do you need to be more on guard in order to protect yourself and your loved ones?

TIED ON

PRAYER

Lord, help me to ride shotgun in my family and be on guard against Satan's schemes. Help me to stand firm in my faith and protect those I love. It's in your holy name I pray, Amen.

WEEK 35

THE BIG DRIVE

MATTHEW 28:16-20

Then the eleven disciples went to Galilee, to the mountain where Jesus had told them to go. When they saw him, they worshiped him; but some doubted. Then Jesus came to them and said, "All authority in heaven and on earth has been given to me. Therefore go and make disciples of all nations, baptizing them in the name of the Father and of the Son and of the Holy Spirit, and teaching them to obey everything I have commanded you. And surely I am with you always, to the very end of the age."

Living in NW Oklahoma means I'm not too far from the Texas panhandle. That said, each spring I have the honor of going to West Texas and working with (in my humble opinion) some of the best cowboys on the planet. My good friend Marshall Long manages the *IV Ranch* and I love working with him and the rest of his crew 'cause not

TIED ON

only are they great hands, but they do things the cowboy way. Each morning before daylight we leave out horseback and ride in a single file line to the back of the pasture. Once we've made it to the backside Marshall starts dropping off cowboys, staggering them out so that we can cover the whole pasture and not miss any cows. A good cow boss like Marshall knows each cowboy well enough to know who can handle being dropped off first and who needs to stay closer to him 'cause they don't know the pasture and could get lost (especially if it's foggy). Once each cowboy is dropped off, all of us start riding slowly back in the direction of the pens—side-winding across the pasture looking for cattle. In our neck of the woods, this is what you call a *drive* and on the IV Ranch, where some pastures are over 2,600 acres, a drive can be pretty big. Once the drive has been made and the pairs are at the pens, the ranch hands work every cow and calf to help assure that they grow and live a long healthy life!

Just like cowboys make a drive gathering cattle that need worked, Christians are called to find and gather men and women that need Jesus. You may be thinking, "Where do we go to find and gather the lost?" Well today's verse tells us, "Therefore go and make disciples of all nations…" This verse shows us that we are to go into "all nations," which implies the whole world. That's a big drive! But as Christ followers, we can't get held up in our own lit-

THE BIG DRIVE

tle Christian corrals and expect to find any people that need to experience the loving works of Jesus. You may be thinking, "I'm not too familiar with how to go about gathering others." Well thankfully, just like a good cow boss, God knows where to drop us off so that we can get people back to Him. Our commitment should be to ride out into this dark and desperate world and start the drive!

CHEW ON THIS
Are you riding the big circle with Christ, gathering up those who need to hear about Him? What pastures has God called you to ride for Him? What other believers do you know that you can ride with on this big circle?

PRAYER
Lord, help me to ride a circle and gather the lost up for you. Help me to introduce them to your forgiveness and salvation and help them to fall in love with your Word so that they can live a godly life for you. In Jesus name I pray, Amen.

WEEK 36

SAVED BY THE CAKE WAGON

JOHN 8:12

When Jesus spoke again to the people, he said, "I am the light of the world. Whoever follows me will never walk in darkness, but will have the light of life."

One day this past spring, me and about twelve other cowboys showed up to help work a bunch of calves at a ranch in West Texas. We showed up knowing that rain was in the forecast. Sure enough, after waiting for an hour or so, the owner decided we'd probably not get much done cause the calves were wet and wouldn't take a brand very well, and more rain was coming. Not wanting to waste the drive getting there, a few of us decided we'd try and find some cows we had missed the day before. So, we road in

SAVED BY THE CAKE WAGON

the dark to the back of the pasture where Marshall, the cow boss, dropped me and some other cowboys off to hopefully find the stray cattle. Well, it wasn't long after he dropped us off, when the rain clouds opened up and the storm hit—and it hit *hard*. It turned pitch black and the lightning was crackin' so close you could feel the hair stand up on the back of your neck. The rain poured down and no other living soul was in sight. I had my horse at a high lope hoping and praying I was headed in the right direction. Then I heard and saw what was music to my ears and beauty to my eyes. It was the siren and the headlights of Marshall's cake wagon. He had made it back to the pickup and was showing us the way home!

In life, we can often find ourselves caught in a storm. All heck has opened up and we don't know which way to go. We feel lost and not sure where to turn. It's in these moments that I'm thankful Jesus is the light that can lead us back home. He is the light of the world and His light shines to show us which way to turn!

Listen to the words of the disciples when they were facing some dark times:

> *"For God, who said, "Let there be light in the darkness," has made this light shine in our hearts so we could know the glory of God that is seen in the face of Jesus Christ."*

TIED ON

We are hard pressed on every side, but not crushed; perplexed, but not in despair; persecuted, but not abandoned; struck down, but not destroyed."
                              −2 Corinthians 4:6,8-9 (NLT)

CHEW ON THIS
Do you find yourself in a storm today? Maybe it's the storm of your failures and bad choices? Are you feeling pressed on every side? Ask God to turn His headlights on and show you the way out of the dark.

PRAYER
God, I need you to shine your light in my dark pasture so that I can find my way home. Please turn on your headlights so that I can see in the dark. It's in your holy name I pray, Amen.

WEEK 37

SAVING THE BEST FOR LAST

GALATIANS 6:4-5
Each one should test their own actions. Then they can take pride in themselves alone, without comparing themselves to someone else, for each one should carry their own load.

It was spring branding time, and I was at the Reed Ranch in Spearman, Texas. Like the years before, we were dropped off at the back of a 6,000-acre pasture before sun up. We had gathered 200 pairs in no time at all, had sorted the mommas off, worked 200 calves, wormed the mommas, stretched out and dehorned three to four momma cows, and sorted off the dries—all before lunch. As we were dragging calves that morning, I thought there was only me and another older cowboy left to drag. Feeling a little cocky, I thought to myself, *"Dang right, they saved the best*

TIED ON

for last—me." Little did I know that there was one more cowboy left that would take the place of the older gentleman that I was dragging with, and his name was none other than Boyd Rice. Boyd is not only a great cowboy, he is a professional horse trainer who has won over three million dollars showing horses in the cutting and working ranch horse pens. In 2014, he was named the "World's Greatest Horseman". Needless to say, my thought of saving the best for last was true, it just wasn't me.

I'll be the first to admit that I'm not the best cowboy to ever throw a leg over a horse, but now I can say I've been in the branding pen with one of the best! I rode out of the pen that morning reveling at the opportunity to have shared the same pen with such a great cowboy.

But then I began to experience something that is painful for me to admit. I caught myself thinking things like, "If I was only as good as him," or "If I could just drag as good as he does," or "If my horses were half as nice as his then I'd really be something." It wasn't until later that I finally realized that I was committing the sin of comparison and I needed to repent of this sin.

You need to understand that not all comparison is wrong. I'll give you an example. When I go to another church, I compare how they do things to how we do things to see if we could improve. I compare their greeters to ours, their facilities to ours. Why? So I can maybe

SAVING THE BEST FOR LAST

take something away from their church that would help us be better in a certain area of our ministry and therefore increase the opportunity to reach more people at our church.

So when does it become wrong to compare? When it steals our joy! You cannot be joyful and envious at the same time. In my story, I found that by comparing myself to Boyd Rice, it was robbing me of my joy and causing me to sin.

So, how do we overcome this sin of comparison? We must realize that God has called us to *do* our best, not always *be* the best. Whether it's in the branding pen or in the office, we are called by God to do our best and then leave the results up to Him for His Glory!

CHEW ON THIS
Who do you compare yourself with? Is it to improve yourself, or are you envious? Ask God to give you the strength to do your best even though you may not be the best at what you're doing.

PRAYER
God, help me to not let comparing myself to others steal my joy. Help me do my best and know that the rest is up to you. It's in your holy name I pray, Amen.

WEEK 38

TAKE GROUND

JOSHUA 1:9
Have I not commanded you? Be strong and courageous. Do not be terrified; do not be discouraged for the Lord your God will be with you wherever you go.

As I've already mentioned in an earlier devo—I love the movie *Tombstone*. The gun fights are some of my favorite scenes. In the famous gunfight at the OK Corral we watch Wyatt Earp and his brothers step forward in the face of danger as they go up against the outlaw gang known as *The Cowboys*. The gang was led by Curly Bill. In the scene some of the outlaw gang is killed, but not all of them. There's a famous scene where Wyatt, played by Kurt Douglass, spares the life of one of the gang leaders know as Ike Clanton. He does this so that Ike can go tell the others that, "Wyatt Earp is now a U.S. Marshal and he's bringing the thunder!" He says, "Tell all the other curs, the law is

TAKE GROUND

comin'. You tell them I'm comin! And hell's comin' with me!" Then Wyatt and his posse scour the region, ridding it of anyone who wears a red sash—the symbol of *The Cowboys*.

Like Wyatt and his famous brothers, we are called to be men of courage, and take ground back from the devil. For far too long, the devil has taken what God says is rightfully ours—he's taken our marriages, our children, and the hearts and minds of our friends. Now is the time that we take courage and fight the good fight for the glory of Jesus Christ. I don't know about you but I'm ready to bring a little hell to the devil, and God is the one who will help us bring it!

As our Scripture for today tells us, we need to have courage! Do you know who our greatest example is of someone who had the courage to take ground? Jesus Christ. It took courage to leave heaven and come to earth. It took courage to be born in a manger, not a palace. It took courage to stand before others and proclaim to be the Savior of the world. It took courage to stand against his enemies and to die on the cross so that we might have eternal life. Jesus Christ is the most courageous man to walk the face of the earth! He not only defended His Father, He took ground for Him. How can we take ground for the Lord? We take a stand against Satan, lead our families to love the Lord, and take advantage of opportuni-

TIED ON

ties to share Jesus with the lost!

CHEW ON THIS
What areas of your life do you need to take back ground for Christ? How can you be more courageous for the Lord?

PRAYER
Lord, help me to take a stand for you. Help me to stand firm in my faith so that I can resist the devil and he will flee from me. Thank you for being with me every step of the way. It's in your holy name I pray, Amen.

WEEK 39

THE BULL RIDER'S ARMOR

EPHESIANS 6:13-17

Therefore put on the full armor of God, so that when the day of evil comes, you may be able to stand your ground, and after you have done everything, to stand. Stand firm then, with the belt of truth buckled around your waist, with the breastplate of righteousness in place, and with your feet fitted with the readiness that comes from the gospel of peace. In addition to all this, take up the shield of faith, with which you can extinguish all the flaming arrows of the evil one. Take the helmet of salvation and the sword of the Spirit, which is the word of God.

If you've ever been to the rodeo, I think you would agree that the most exciting event at the rodeo is the bull rid-

TIED ON

ing. Why? Cause it's nail-biting to watch a wiry cowboy who most commonly weighs less than a couple hundred pounds, get on a bull that can weigh up to 2,500 pounds of pure muscle. Because the bulls are so powerful and dangerous, most bull riders have gone to wearing protective gear to lessen the chance of them getting seriously injured. I'll tell you something that I've never seen before when it comes to bull riding. I've never seen a bull rider nod their head, bust out of the chute, and then say, *"Throw me my helmet."* That would be dumb because at that point it would be too late. If they were to get hit in the face by a horn without their helmet on, it would be too late!

Like bull riders, we are told to put on the full armor of God to protect us from our powerful enemy, the Devil—and we, too, must have it on *before* we face the enemy. Why? So we can be prepared for the nasty ride that we often find ourselves in with the Devil! Like the bull rider, we all want to make a successful ride in this life. We all want to live victoriously for Christ, but we can only do this when we put on the full armor of God. We are going to face temptation and we are going to fight battles with sin and if we are to win those battles each day, we have to be protected and armed for battle!

THE BULL RIDER'S ARMOR

CHEW ON THIS
Do you put your spiritual armor on each day? What part of the Armor of God (remember, there are six pieces) do you feel like you forget to put on most days? Are you prepared to fight the battles in life with the weapons found in the word of God?

PRAYER
Lord, remind me to put on your armor each day. Protect my mind, my heart, and my life. Help me to be prepared for the battles I will face. It's in your holy name I pray, Amen.

WEEK 40

THE BUCKLE

JAMES 1:12
... [he] will receive the crown of life that God has promised to those who love him.

Being a cowboy who likes to compete at ranch rodeos and also put on ranch rodeos through our cowboy church, I've learned that sometimes more than winning money, a true cowboy would rather win a handmade champion buckle. For many cowboys it's not the fame or fortune they're after, but the pride and honor of being a champion at something they do every day.

Like the cowboy, I believe that as Christians we are called not to focus on the fame and fortune of this world, but on the crown we will receive from our father in heaven if we've place our faith in Jesus and served Him well.

THE BUCKLE

God's "crown of life," or buckle if you will, is not glory and honor here on earth, but the reward of eternal life in heaven. A believer's buckle is eternal life! It's fun to receive "earthly crowns" but we need to make sure our eyes are set on the one true champion buckle—eternal life.

CHEW ON THIS
In what ways can you focus more on the eternal, rather than on earthly things? Are you living for the championship buckle that will never rust?

PRAYER
Lord, forgive me where I have focused more on earthly things, than on eternal things. Help me to share with someone how to receive the ultimate buckle, eternal life in heaven! It's in your holy name I pray, Amen.

WEEK 41

THE CORNER POST

HEBREWS 11:1
Now faith is confidence in what we hope for and assurance about what we do not see.

When you build a fence, it usually takes a whole lot of supplies. These supplies may include wire, fence stretchers, a tamping tool, line posts, and if you want to really dress the fence up, wood. However, the most essential part of the fence is the corner post. A good corner post may be anywhere from 6" to 12" round and can be anywhere from 8' to 10' tall. When it comes to setting a corner you typically put at least 1/3 of the post in the ground. Why? Because the corner post is what makes or breaks a fence. If it's not firm and solid, the whole fence will be affected!

THE CORNER POST

Similar to how the corner post is essential to building a fence that will last, we are called to live a corner-post Christian life. We are to set our lives deep in the things of the Lord. Things like being grounded in God's Word and firmly planted in a growing church. Also we must have faith. What is faith? Just like the fence whose strength is found in what you can't see in the ground, our faith works the same way.

Faith isn't what you see on the outside, it's what's not seen that makes it faith. You can have a corner post that is really straight above the ground, it can be really big around, and it can be soaked in cresol so it won't rot, but if it's not set deep in the ground, it's not going to last! But if that corner post is set deep in a hole that is well tamped or set in concrete, it will be strong and withstand whatever comes against it. If a cow tries to run through the fence, it will stand firm. In the same way, faith is what's in the ground! And faith is what will make us firm, solid, corner-post Christians! My desire—and I pray it's yours too—is that our faith would be planted deeply in Christ!

CHEW ON THIS
Are you living a corner-post Christian life? Is your faith ready to withstand whatever life hits it with?

TIED ON

PRAYER

Lord, increase my faith. Help me live a corner-post Christian life with a faith that is deeply rooted. It's in Your holy name I pray, Amen.

WEEK 42

THE FLY OF LIFE

1 CORINTHIANS 16:14
Do everything in love.

If you've ever stayed out on a Chuckwagon you know that every wagon has what they call a "fly". This "fly" is a canvas like tarp that goes over the bows of the wagon to help protect everything that is important to the cowboys that are there working and the cook. Once camp is set, this fly can also be stretched out over the entire camp. From the bedrolls, to the food, to the saddles and gear, the fly provides much needed protection. Not to mention, it keeps the sun from beating down on the cowboys after a long hard day of work. It's also waterproof and keeps everything dry. The fly protects everything.

TIED ON

Just like how the fly on a Chuckwagon covers and protects all that a cowboy holds dear, *love* should be the "fly" of life. Every decision we make should be covered with love. Every response we give should be covered with love. If we're going reach people for Christ, we must cover them in love! If our friends are ever going to be motivated to come back to church, or have a personal relationship with Christ, then we must cover them with the love of Christ. Love is the *fly* of life!

CHEW ON THIS
Is love the cover that you use for everything you do? Who do you need to show the love of Christ so that they can know Him personally? What are some ways that you can cover others with love?

PRAYER
Lord, help me to cover everything I do in love. Help my words and actions show your love to others. It's in your holy name I pray, Amen.

WEEK 43

THE GREAT HANDLER

1 JOHN 5:12
He who has the Son has life; he who does not have the Son of God does not have life. (NASB)

At our cowboy church we strive to use events that relate to the cowboy culture to reach our culture for Christ. One of those events is our Cowdog trials. At our trial, the Cowdog (with a little help from the handler/dog owner), must ever so gently push all the cattle through an obstacle course in the fastest amount of time. Every time we've had a trial I'm amazed at the control these handlers have on their dogs. Obviously the handlers who had more control of their dog did better than the one who didn't have that much control. The dogs that got distracted or didn't

TIED ON

listen to their handler's commands had to overcome even more obstacles because of their lack of obedience. Some dogs had a mind of their own and they acted out, made a move, or got a hold when they shouldn't have. But the dogs that listened and obeyed their handler won! Not to mention it's a true thing of beauty to watch them work!

As followers of Jesus Christ, we must ask the question, "How do we allow the Great Handler (God) to have control of our lives?" The answer to this question starts with us knowing Him personally. To get into the Cowdog business, every Cowdog owner has to start by buying a good dog or two to begin their program. Most good Cowdogs aren't cheap, costing thousands of dollars. Christ paid it all to purchase us. See, although Christ created us, he doesn't own us until we surrender ownership over to Him. He bought us with the price of His own blood, but we have to accept His price and give Him our lives.

Once we know Christ personally, the Holy Spirit also must have a handle on our lives. The Holy Spirit is our counselor and our guide. We receive the Holy Spirit once we are saved. How do we allow the Holy Spirit to have a handle on us? We live by the Spirit, not our sinful nature! Cowdogs have two options—they can listen to their handler and have success, or they can ignore their handler, do things their own way and fail. We also have the same choice—we can allow our sinful nature to have a handle

THE GREAT HANDLER

on our lives, or we can live by the Spirit and allow Him to have a handle on our lives!

CHEW ON THIS
What kind of handle does God have on you? Are you listening to the Holy Spirit and walking in obedience to Him right now or are you ignoring His commands and following your own way?

PRAYER
Lord, thank you for purchasing me with your own blood. I want you to have a handle on my life. Help me to walk in step with you and be led by the Holy Spirit. Show me areas of my life where I'm not walking in step with you and lead me back into a right relationship with you. It's in your holy name I pray, Amen.

WEEK 44

THE ORDINARY COWBOY

1 SAMUEL 16:11
So he asked Jesse, "Are these all the sons you have?" "There is still the youngest," Jesse answered. "He is tending the sheep." Samuel said, "Send for him; we will not sit down until he arrives."

A lot of times I'll meet some great cowboys while working calves, and when they find out that I'm a preacher, they often times go to acting like they aren't worth much to the Lord. They say things like, "I'm just a cowboy. I don't have much to offer God. I just do my thing and hope God uses it for something."

Like many of these cowboys, King David didn't come from a high palace, he came from the pasture. David was a shepherd. It was a dirty, unwanted job that most people wouldn't think would produce a king. God saw differently. When speaking to David's father, God said that David was chosen to be the one—the next king of Israel.

You might think: "Well, I'm just a pumper, I just work for the county, I'm just a cowboy, I'm just a farmer, or I'm just a mom. God can't use little ole me!" But the truth is, He can! And He will if you have a heart for Him. You may believe the lie that you aren't qualified, but, here's an important truth: God doesn't call the qualified, He qualifies the called!

You might be reading this and thinking that God can't use you. You may be thinking, "I don't know enough, I don't live well enough, I haven't been a Christian long enough, I'm too young, I'm too old." I challenge you to take your eyes off yourself and put your eyes on God. Listen, God can use anyone who is willing to love Him with all their heart! God didn't choose David because of his qualifications, He chose him because he had a heart for Him!

CHEW ON THIS

What have you not done for the Lord cause you felt you weren't qualified enough?

TIED ON

PRAYER

Lord, use ordinary me to do extraordinary things for you. Help me have a heart for you and a heart to change the world. It's in your holy name I pray, Amen.

WEEK 45

THE PERFORMANCE HORSE

MATTHEW 9:12-13
On hearing this, Jesus said, "It is not the healthy who need a doctor, but the sick. But go and learn what this means: 'I desire mercy, not sacrifice.'"

When you think of a performance horse, you would be right to think of a horse that performs. These horses are bred and trained to perform certain maneuvers, patterns, or jobs for a score by the judges or the fastest time. In this industry, all that really matters is how well the horse performs. If the horse doesn't perform well, then there are no earnings or trophies, and if the horse does perform well then it can be a very lucrative business, not only in the show ring, but in the breeding shed as well.

While this is fine for the performance horse... we sadly

TIED ON

find this same performance-based mentality existing in many of our churches as well. At some point we lose sight of the fact that God's love is not dependent on our performance, but His mercy. This isn't so much of a problem when we first give our lives to Christ because we do things out of love and knowledge of His mercy and grace we've received. But over time our relationship becomes based more on how we perform and we lose sight of what is most important to God. Sure serving in the church, reading the bible, attending church, and tithing are all things we should be committed to, but in today's verse we see that God desires something more. He desires mercy and for us to receive His mercy and offer that same mercy to others.

CHEW ON THIS

Have you received God's mercy and given Him your heart? Do you get caught up in trying to perform for Christ and lose sight of what He really desires? God says to each of us, "I care less about your performance, and I care more about you receiving and remembering my mercy and giving my mercy away!"

PRAYER

God, thank you for your amazing mercy! Please help me to both accept it and give it away, and may it all be for your glory. It's in your holy name I pray, Amen.

WEEK 46

THE REAL MCCOY

PSALM 112:1
Praise the LORD! Blessed is the man who fears the LORD, who greatly delights in his commandments! (ESV)

There are a lot of stories about the origin of the phrase, "the real McCoy." but if someone has ever called you the real McCoy, then you're generally known as the "real deal" or the "genuine article". Tom Moorhouse and his brothers are fifth generation Texas cattlemen. Tom is just bent the cowboy way. I had the pleasure of meeting Tom a few years ago and from what I've learned about him—being handy with a horse, not knowing the word quit, and the way he would rather sleep out on the chuckwagon in his bedroll than in his bed at home—I would say that Tom is the real McCoy!

When it comes to living the Christian life, I believe that God wants us to be the real McCoy. He wants us to be

TIED ON

bent His way, to have grit, and to be sold out to His way of living. How do we do this? One way we become the real McCoy for Christ, is to follow His Word.

Everything we need to know about life can be found in the Bible. From its pages we can learn how to live, how to make the right decisions, and how to raise a godly family. Some will say, "I read it but I don't understand it." Well, if you don't have a Bible that is easy to understand, then I would encourage you to get a version (NIV/NLT) that is easier to read. Some would say, "I never have it with me when I have time to actually read it." I always tell them to "get it on your phone!" If you're like me, you always have your phone with you. My father's single greatest impact on me was seeing him get up every morning, drink a cup of raw eggs and honey (yes just like Rocky Balboa), sit down in his recliner, turn the weather channel on silent, and read his bible. My dad was and still is the real McCoy, and by his example I want to be the real McCoy too.

CHEW ON THIS

What do you think it looks like for you to be the real McCoy? How can you set the example for your family to become the real McCoy for Christ? When was the last time your kids saw you reading God's Word?

THE REAL MCCOY

PRAYER

Lord, give me a hunger for your Word. Help me to be the genuine article, when it comes to my relationship with you. Show me what it looks like to be the real McCoy! It's in your holy name I pray, Amen.

WEEK 47

LIFE'S A TWITCH

EXODUS 14:13-14
But Moses told the people, "Don't be afraid. Just stand still and watch the Lord rescue you today. The Egyptians you see today will never be seen again. The Lord himself will fight for you. Just stay calm." (NLT)

When it comes to using a twitch on a horse, folks that don't understand it would probably think that it is a cruel tool that hurts the animal. They would be mistaken. When a twitch is used properly, it triggers the release of endorphins from the horse's brain, producing a calming effect. Sure, the horse may fight it for a few short seconds, but just like sedation, the less he fights the quicker it works. One reason for using a twitch would be a horse that has suffered a cut on its leg, and it won't let the owner dress the wound. This would be a case for when the owner or veterinarian would use the twitch to get the horse to calm down and stand still long enough to get him cleaned up and doctored. Twitching is not only safer for the horse, but it's safer for the handler as well.

In the same way that a person uses a twitch to calm a horse, God uses the twitches of life to quiet us. Illness, loss, failure, trials, temptation, tribulation, and even our enemies, are all examples of twitches that God might use to get us quiet and willing. Like it or not, these twitches are inevitable. However, though uncomfortable for a little while, the twitches of life release our faith and trust in God, helping us learn to handle life with a peace and calmness that can only come from Him. We would be smart to learn from the horse that quickly calms down and stands still and realize that the quicker we get quiet before God, the quicker we can experience his powerful provision and care. More often than not, God doesn't take the twitch off until it produces the quiet trust He wants it to—no matter how long it takes. In many cases the longer we resist, the longer the twitch will remain.

CHEW ON THIS

What types of twitches does God have on you? Have you learned to be quiet, or are you still thrashing around? Memorize Psalm 46:10, which says, "Be still, and know that I am God..."

TIED ON

PRAYER
God, thank you for the twitches of life. Thank you for the lessons you teach me through them and for rescuing me from them. Even though they are uncomfortable, I know you use them to strengthen my faith and trust in you. Please help me to not fight them, but to be quiet and still before you. It's in your holy name I pray, Amen.

WEEK 48

THE WINDMILL

JOHN 7:38

Whoever believes in me, as the Scripture has said, streams of living water will flow from within him.

Chances are, you've probably seen a windmill. In order for a windmill to work, the wind has to blow and the pump has to pump so the water can come up from the ground and fill the tank, and your livestock can have something to drink. My wife's great grandparents put in the windmill at our house. Not only did they use it to water their livestock, but being the forward thinking people that they were, they put in an overflow drain and piped a line from the tank to their garden. They did this so that when the tank got full, it would flow down the pipe and into the rows where the plants were planted and they could grow some great homegrown produce.

TIED ON

As I see it, we are asked by God to do the same thing. God has called us to be a windmill that pumps His living water up for us to drink from, but we're also called to be the pipe that God pumps the living water through to a thirsty world. Maybe you already look for opportunities to pour out the love of Jesus at work, at school, or at home—in that case, keep up the good work! But maybe you've tasted the cleansing water that Jesus has filled your tank with, but you haven't allowed Jesus' living water to flow out of you and into the lives of others so that they too can drink of His goodness. What a tragedy it is for us as Christians to experience the refreshing goodness of Jesus Christ but never allow His goodness to flow *through* our lives to those who are desperately thirsty for something more! Understand this—it's our privilege, our calling, and our duty to be God's windmill!

CHEW ON THIS
How full is your tank of Christ's living water? Are you a windmill that allows God to pump living water through so that others may drink of God's goodness, love, and salvation? Who does God want you to pump living water into?

PRAYER
Lord, help me to share with others what you've done in my

THE WINDMILL

life. Give me the boldness to open my mouth and proclaim your goodness so that the world may taste of your living water! It's in your holy name I pray, Amen.

WEEK 49

WHAT A TOOL

EPHESIANS 2:10
For we are God's handiwork, created in Christ Jesus to do good works, which God prepared in advance for us to do.

In the cowboy culture, there are many useful tools to better get a job done. One example is chaps *(pronounced shaps).* Some types of chaps include chinks (which come done just below the knee), shotguns (which are chaps that come all the way done the leg and have a zipper all the way down as well), Batwings (which are a style of chap that have a wider rounded bottom to them), and Woolies (which are usually a shotgun style chap that has sheep or goat hair on the outside to keep a cowboy warm). The purpose of wearing chaps is to protect your legs. Chaps provide protection from things like sharp limbs and thorns, they lessen the blow when a calf kicks

WHAT A TOOL

you, and they help keep you from getting a shot of blackleg when your buddy who's giving shots misses the calf and ends up poking you. Needless to say, chaps are a vital tool in a cowboy's line of business.

There are two definitions for the word "tool": 1) something useful for a distinct purpose (i.e. chaps), and 2) the negative slang word for a fool. The latter definition may describe a person who feels worthless or useless 'cause someone has told them they are or they just don't believe in themselves. You may find yourself feeling like a tool/fool today. God wants you to know that you were not created by Him to be a fool, but to be a useful tool for His glory. When we surrender our lives to Jesus, we go from being a "tool" (fool) to being a tool that is accepted, worthy, and useful to God. Just like chaps are designed for a purpose, we are designed by God to fulfill His purpose. You may be asking, "What's my purpose?" Our purpose is to know God and make Him known. As today's verse shows us we are also called *to do good works*. Works are what show that our faith is for real and not to mention they show the world the power of God to use ordinary people to do extraordinary things!

CHEW ON THIS
What kind of tool are you? Do you feel useless and unwor-

TIED ON

thy today or are you being used by God as a tool to make Him known? Examine your heart and turn to God to find your worth today, and commit to allowing Him to use you as His tool!

PRAYER

God, thank you for having a purpose for me! I want to know you, worship you, and do good works so others will come to know you as well. Please show me my purpose and help me to be a useful tool for you. It's in your holy name I pray, Amen.

WEEK 50

WHAT MAKES YOUR CLOTHES FALL OFF

GALATIANS 3:26-27

You are all sons of God through faith in Christ Jesus, for all of you who were baptized into Christ have clothed yourselves with Christ (NASB).

Cowboys sometimes get a bad rap for not having style or not being fashionable. But I don't think that is true at all. Cowboys have just as much style as anybody else. From the hat styles they wear—felt, straw, and palm leaf with 4" to 5" brims, creases like the cattlemen's crease, the puncher, and the Gus, to the taco, and flat brim buckaroo style brims. They have all kinds of style in the jeans they wear—Wranglers, Levis, Arait, Stetson, and 20x. They also wear all styles of boots—from Beck's, to Leddy's, Justin, Boulet, and Twisted X. They wear shirts from

TIED ON

Schafer, to Cinch, to Panhandle Slim, with pearl snaps or buttons. The jean jacket is a cowboy staple and many wear colorful wild rags to show off their style and flare. While you don't find many cowboys talking style, they do have it and they like to show it off!

Today's verse says that those who have believed in Christ, *"have clothed yourselves with Christ"*. What does it mean to be *"clothed in Christ"*? It means that because Christ has made his home in us, we are able to clothe ourselves with supernatural compassion, kindness, humility, forgiveness, and above all, love!

The Joe Nichols song, "Tequila Makes Her Clothes Fall Off" is about a gal who drinks too many margaritas and starts taking all her clothes off. For this gal, it was alcohol that made her clothes fall off. Spiritually speaking, what makes your clothes fall off? What makes you lose your compassion for people? What makes you lose your love for others? What temptation is it that causes you to want to pull off Christ and put the old clothes of sin back on? Maybe your clothes of Christ start falling off when you are hanging out with a certain crowd. Maybe it's because you are surrounded with people you just can't stand and they cause you to just lose it. Listen, if you are truly saved, then you have the power in Christ to not lose your spiritual clothes.

WHAT MAKES YOUR CLOTHES FALL OFF

CHEW ON THIS
What makes your clothes of Christ fall off? What do you need to change in order to remain *clothed in Christ*?

PRAYER
Lord, clothe me with your compassion, humility and love. Show me what makes these clothes fall off and help me to not put the clothes of sin back on. It's in your holy name I pray, Amen.

WEEK 51

YOU CAN LEAD A HORSE TO WATER

JOHN 7:37B-38

If anyone is thirsty, let him come to me and drink. Whoever believes in me, as the Scripture has said, streams of living water will flow from within him.

I'm sure you've heard the phrase, "You can lead a horse to water, but you can't make him drink." The other day I went out to catch one of our horses and noticed that her water tank was completely empty. Apparently my kids had failed to do all of their chores. After turning the hydrant on to fill the tank, I haltered one of our horses to get her saddled and ready to go to a ranch rodeo. After getting her saddled, I went back to turn off the water and offer my horse a drink, but she wouldn't take one. I thought to myself, there is absolutely no way that I can

YOU CAN LEAD A HORSE TO WATER

make her drink! I know she needs to drink, and soon she will wish she had, but apparently she wasn't thirsty enough.

Well, the same is true in life! Jesus Christ offers us living water, but he doesn't make us drink! What is this living water? It's an abundant life on earth and an eternal life in heaven. But like a horse won't drink until he's thirsty, many people must be thirsty before they will choose to take a drink of the living water. Being spiritually thirsty means that you long for something more than this world has to offer. You realize that you have a void in your life that can't be filled by anything in this world. It is at this point that your spiritual drink is the living water that Jesus offers! What does it mean to drink? It means we believe in Him. We take in His grace! We enter into a trusting, ongoing relationship with Christ! When we drink the living water, He fills our life with His Holy Spirit. He washes us clean from the inside out. Many of you have taken a drink by making Him the Lord of your life. You've tasted the refreshing water that the Lord gives and you have found true life. I encourage you to drink more and more everyday so that you can be refreshed and ready to go to work for the Lord! But maybe you realize that you have been offered the living water but you have yet to drink. Don't be stubborn any longer. Drink up!

TIED ON

CHEW ON THIS

Are you thirsty to receive more out of life? Have you taken a drink of the living water? Who do you know that is thirsty and needs to be offered a drink?

PRAYER

Lord, thank you for making it so easy to quench our thirst. Thank you for offering us living water that truly satisfies. I accept your offer and I want to drink up your living water. Also, Lord, help me to share your water with others I know. It's in your holy name I pray, Amen.

WEEK 52

GETTING A LITTLE WESTERN

PSALM 145:3
"Great is the LORD and most worthy of praise; his greatness no one can fathom."

When a cowboy says, "It got a little western," it usually means that things got exciting. For instance, when a cowboy gets on a cold-backed colt in the brisk morning air and the colt splits in two—things just got a little western. Or when a momma cow decides to turn and fight instead of running off—things are fixin' to get western. It's in these moments, that if a concerned mother is around, they gasp and run to protect their baby boy. But if things get a little western in a pen full of cowboys, their response is usually a hardy whoop, holler, and cheer!

TIED ON

When things get a little western, most cowboys respond with pure enjoyment (at least until you have to go to be taken to the hospital)!

Like a cowboy enjoys it when things get a little western, I believe that God enjoys watching us have the same response to the exciting things He has done. Worship of God isn't just singing—it should be something we express out of our love and devotion in every area of our lives. Truth is, we can worship anything. People, things, sports, even our kids can all be worshipped. You may be thinking, "How do I know if I'm wrongfully worshiping something?" The answer would be: When you find yourself constantly neglecting the things of God to do something, own something, or follow someone besides Jesus. If you haven't prayed in weeks, if you haven't been to church in four months, if you haven't read your Bible in a year—you may be worshipping something else.

Jesus should be the object of our worship. Why? Because of who He is and what He has done. He created us. His name is above every name. He died for our sins. He paid a debt that we couldn't pay, and His love is unconditional. And to top it all off, He did all of this while we were still sinners (Romans 5:8).

Our response should be to get a little western for Him. In other words we should gratefully, passionately, and enthusiastically express our praise daily and in church!

GETTING A LITTLE WESTERN

CHEW ON THIS
Is Jesus the object of your worship or has something else taken His place? When was the last time that you enthusiastically expressed your praise to God?

PRAYER
Lord I want to get a little western for you. Help me to freely express my love for you and help others to see the passion I have for you as I live my life in worship! It's in your holy name I pray, Amen.

NOTES

NOTES

NOTES

NOTES

NOTES